True Tales

Buried Trea

By EDWARD ROWE SN

Author of SECRETS OF THE NORTH ATLANTIC ISLANDS, *Etc.*

Illustrated with Photographs, Maps and Diagrams

THIS is a rare item! Doubloons and pieces of eight! It is a book of nothing but true stories concerning buried treasure.

Edward Rowe Snow leads you to fabulous Oak Island, Nova Scotia, where over $400,000 has been spent in vain to find a treasure worth $10,000,000; to the West Indies, where Sir William Phips found over a million on a sunken treasure ship; to a treasure cave where Pirate Morgan buried his loot; to Bermuda, where many fabulous treasures have been uncovered. The author also reveals no less than sixty individual authentic treasure finds up and down the Atlantic coast, and suggests many more locations where treasure can be discovered.

You will be amazed at the story concerning the chimney's secret and the account of Fisherman Doane's Lucky Night will intrigue you. Mr. Snow tells of a treasure map which actually worked and also gives you his story of the baffling hoard of the treasure ship *Whidah,* still buried just offshore under the white sands of Cape Cod. The adventures which befell the Byfield Buccaneers should induce everyone to go out and dig for treasure, while his account of sunken ships offers alluring hope for substantial treasure for all of us to be found at the bottom of the sea.

The last chapter in the book is a true presentation of the author's discovery of buried treasure back in 1945, a discovery so unusual and interesting that the account of it appeared in a subsequent issue of *Time* Magazine and also in *Reader's Digest.*

An ageless book

DODD, MEAD & COMPANY

TRUE TALES OF BURIED TREASURE

TRUE TALES OF

BURIED TREASURE

by

EDWARD ROWE SNOW

ILLUSTRATED WITH PHOTOGRAPHS AND MAPS

1952

Dodd, Mead & Company

New York

Published November, 1951
Second printing, December, 1951
Third printing, March, 1952

15498

TO

Dorothy Caroline Snow
our greatest treasure

Introduction

BURIED treasure always appeals to the adventuresome spirit in each of us. Indeed, there are few people who have not thrilled at the chance of finding a vast hoard of gold or silver buried somewhere along a great sandy sea-beach or deep in an inland glen, far from the roar of the mighty ocean.

Treasure, possibly hidden in the earth or sand by some famous pirate, may be awaiting the turn of your shovel to uncover it. You never know when you may be on the verge of an important discovery, for it may come at the most unexpected time or place. Always be alert for that discovery.

However, it is best for me to put forward a friendly warning. Although in this volume you will read of millions of dollars recovered from land and sea, every one of them believed to be true stories, it is naturally impossible for all those who seek it to find buried treasure. In fact, for each of us who has found or will find buried treasure there are a thousand searchers destined to be unlucky and never discover any.

On the other hand, far too many treasure seekers, because of their acceptance of the fact that the average searcher will never discover gold or silver hoards, give up their efforts after a few disappointments. How often I have received letters from them, admitting their failures. They have begun to wonder if anyone ever really found buried treasure at all. This book is the answer to their doubt, for in these pages I have chosen over fifty true stories from almost 600 which I investigated, true stories about the finding of buried treasure. Furthermore, I have made it possible for anyone reading these pages to hold pirate treasure in his hand merely by making a visit to Boston, Massachusetts, where in the Marine Museum of the Old State House I have deposited a genuine pirate piece of eight, with instructions that it may be shown to and handled by any visitor who asks for it.

Actually, treasure has been discovered all over this country, in every state of the union! I have hundreds of authenticated cases involving substantial sums discovered up and down this Atlantic Coast and inland for hundreds of miles. Without question, for every case which has been discovered there are at least two others which my efforts failed to find.

In my possession I have pieces of eight, doubloons, American gold coins and silver dollars, not from one or two treasures but from a total of nine treasure hoards. The true stories of each of these I include in this book, together with many photographs of various treasure coins.

If you ever do get discouraged while hunting for treasure, never forget that in the last 350 years millions of dollars in gold and silver have been recovered from their hiding places, and that someone had to find them. It is inevitable that many more millions will be discovered in this New World because of the improvement in techniques, and you may as well be the person who discovers them.

In eleven years, because of my intense interest in treasure and because of stories I have told in my lectures or over the air, I have received the rather monumental total of 43,000 letters and communications about hidden gold and silver. Some of these communications are almost unbelievable in what they tell, indicating an incredible faith in metal detectors, dreams, hunches, and strange signs.

Although it is often the casual treasure seeker who finds the treasure, I do think that for those of you who go after your objective in a purely scientific manner there is more hope of finding treasure. With determination, perseverance and a fair amount of luck it may be YOU who will discover the hidden hoard.

As I write these words, definite evidence keeps coming to me that treasure is still being buried and still being found every month of the year in this country and in various other parts of the North American continent.

For this volume I have chosen the most interesting true stories concerning treasure I have come across. The last chapter contains my own tale of buried treasure, and I trust that before completing the chapter you will try to solve the code which led to my discovery of a pirate hoard at Cape Cod.

It is my hope that some day one of my readers will find a substantial quantity of gold doubloons or pieces of eight, possibly because of an inspiration he or she may have obtained from the pages of this book. In any case, my advice for all treasure seekers is to go ahead and follow whatever clues this book or your own research may suggest. My continuous word of warning is that you should never be discouraged by failure, and never expect success. Then if you don't find the treasure, you will not be too disappointed, and if you are successful, you'll be able to stand it more gracefully. Keep everlastingly at it, however.

To each of my readers, when you go out in search of buried treasure, I wish the best of luck. Feel free to write me at any time about what you may be planning or what you have accomplished. I'll be interested.

EDWARD ROWE SNOW

Marshfield, Massachusetts
June 7, 1951

Contents

Illustrations

Sketches and drawings

Photographs following Page 48

Illustrations

Sketches and drawings

Photographs following Page 48

Airplane view of Oak Island

Collection of pirate gold and silver

The author with metal detector

John Light, New England's youngest diver

Walter Wynant

The author about to descend into ruined cabin

Cross-sectional view of pirate ship in harbor

Material from wreck

Charred fragments of color

TRUE TALES OF BURIED TREASURE

CHAPTER 1

The Greatest of Them All

ON A farm in Monsweag, Maine, in the year 1661, a ten-year-old boy was planning his future. His name was Bill Phips, and he was the son of a mother and father who eventually brought up a family of twenty-six children. As our story opens, Bill is telling his brother of his desire to go to sea.

"I'll first learn to be a ship carpenter, and in a few years I can build my own vessels. Later I'll sail my own ships up and down this coast. Then, if I can find out where it is, I'd like most of all to go after some of that Spanish treasure that went down in the ocean around the West Indies!"

At that time the Monsweag farm, located some distance from Wiscasset, Maine, was in a desolate section of the

Maine coast, where the growl of the wild bear, the howl of the wolf, and the war cries of the Indians were often heard.

Bill Phips' dreams of life on the sea had no results at first, for his father put him out sheep herding. Eight years went by, and finally young Phips decided to appeal to his parent.

"Father," young Bill began, "I'm eighteen. I've been faithful here herding sheep, and I've even given up any chance of going to school and learning how to read and write. But I do want to amount to something. Please, sir, let me start in as apprentice over at the shipyard." His father grumbled at first, but then, realizing the fairness of Bill's request, he told the boy he'd think it over. By this time Bill was a young giant, well over six feet in height, and strongly built.

Early the next day his father awakened Bill, and told him he could have his wish. That very noon Bill set out for a shipyard in what is now Bath, Maine, and there, during the following four years, he learned the trade of shipbuilder from beginning to end. In 1673 he was graduated as a full-fledged shipbuilder, and could practice that difficult art whenever he found an occasion for it.

He decided to go to the great seaport of Boston, Massachusetts, which was then the most important town in North America. His mother and father accompanied him to the packet aboard which he was to sail.

When they arrived at the boat, Mrs. Phips said, "Now, William, we'll be awaiting some sort of word from you

It's too bad that you can't write. But you'll do your best to get word to us, won't you, William?"

"Yes, I promise, but I'm going to learn how to write and read soon. You just wait and see."

"Well," responded his father, "you can't learn everything at once. Good luck, Son."

Farewells were said, the sails unfurled, and the tiny Maine packet began the long sea journey to Boston. Bill stood at the taffrail and waved good-bye. At his feet was his small seabag which contained all his worldly possessions, consisting of an extra suit of clothes and a few shillings.

On arriving in Boston, he was overwhelmed at first by the size of the town, but faced with the necessity of earning his own living, he soon sought and obtained employment in the local shipyard. Later he occupied his evenings learning how to read and write. He never was more than passing in either, but he managed to accomplish his purpose.

Not so long afterwards he met a young widow, Mrs. Mary Spencer Hull. According to Cotton Mather, she was a "young gentlewoman of good repute, the daughter of one Roger Spencer." In those days it was considered quite wrong for a young widow to remain single for too long a time after her husband's death, and so, when Bill Phips fell in love with her and proposed marriage, she accepted him almost at once. He was then well over six feet in height, and was built like a wrestler, a fine figure of a man.

His wife, although still comparatively well-to-do, had

recently lost a substantial part of her fortune. Because of his limited means and of her reduced circumstances, they moved into a place of meager accommodations, but Phips soon explained his plans to his young wife.

"Some day we'll leave this dwelling, and we'll move to a mansion more becoming your worth, Mary. Why, I'll be the owner of a fair brick house in the Green Lane of North Boston." Whether or not Mary really felt that this would ever happen, she heartily agreed with him that in time they'd be able to carry out their rosy plans.

A short time later the ambitious young ship builder received a contract to construct a vessel at Monsweag Bay, near his birthplace, and in August, 1676, a beautiful ship slid down the ways into the waters off the Maine coast, with her builder in command, for Bill Phips had learned how to sail a ship as well as how to build one.

During that very month the Indians went on the rampage, and one night they attacked the little community. Everyone in the vicinity fled to the safety of the new ship, which Captain Bill had pushed out into the bay before the Indians could get aboard. He then sailed her to Boston. On his arrival he informed the startled inhabitants of the raid.

Back in Monsweag, the Indians burned down his shipyard and his nearby lumberyard, in which he had invested all his wealth. Eventually the colonists were able to return to Maine to resettle, but Captain Bill was left penniless by the incident. He had no shipyard, no lumber and no money. Indeed, his future appeared bleak. However, there was one big point in his favor. He never became discouraged. Within a week after he learned that his savings had been wiped out, he took his wife aside again.

"Never you mind, Mary. I'll still have that fine brick house in the Green Lane for you. Don't forget."

Again she encouraged him, for there was something in her husband's character which convinced his wife and his friends that he would reach the top some day.

It was shortly afterwards, down on Scarlett's Wharf, that Captain Bill learned of a newcomer at the Boston waterfront who had recently returned from the West Indies. Phips made haste to meet this stranger and to consult him privately at the wharf's counting house.

"I understand," began Phips, "that you have recently returned from the West Indies. Is that correct?"

"That is right, Captain Phips," the sailor answered.

"What did you hear about sunken Spanish ships?"

"Well, sir, I did talk with two Spaniards who had information about treasure galleons which went down in a great storm, but why should I tell you?"

"Why not," countered Phips, "especially when I'll make it worth your while? I'll pay for your time and effort."

"My time may be worth quite a little, Captain Phips, and perhaps it may be too expensive."

"I don't like to bargain around," snapped Phips, who was beginning to lose his temper. "Here's five pounds. Now either tell me what you know or get out!" And so it came about that the sailor told Phips the tale which the two Spaniards had told him.

He explained that in the year 1643 a mighty treasure fleet of Spanish plate galleons with approximately $21,-

000,000 in gold, silver and precious jewels sailed from the West Indies bound for Spain. There were sixteen heavily-laden ships in all and they sailed into the teeth of one of the worst tropical hurricanes ever experienced in West Indian history. One by one the mighty monarchs of the Spanish Empire sank to their doom under the sea, until finally only one surviving galleon remained afloat, the *Santissima Trinidad*.

With superhuman effort and skill gained from long experience at sea, Captain Francis Guerres ran his vessel out of the storm, eluded the dangerous coral reefs of the uncharted seas, and finally came about, returning to Puerto Plata, whence the plate fleet had sailed. The only captain to return, he was exonerated in court of any blame for the disaster which befell the fleet. Meanwhile, the members of his crew, once ashore in the local taverns, told other sailors of the scores of their friends aboard the fifteen lost galleons, sailors who would never return to their families.

Gradually the disaster which befell the plate fleet became known all over the civilized world, wherever men of the sea gathered. By 1650 sailors who knew the facts were passing the word along that fifteen heavily-laden Spanish galleons, bulging with gold and silver, had gone down in the great tempest of November 15, 1643.

And thus it was that Captain Phips heard the details of this remarkable calamity which, as far as was known, had never happened before in the world's history. A fleet worth almost $20,000,000 sunk in the West Indian Ocean!

The former Maine farm boy was thrilled with a great desire to sail at once in search of this fabulous sunken treasure, the finding of which would furnish him with the means to construct the brick house in the Green Lane of North Boston. For the next few years Phips was more active than ever in sailing, cruising and trading. Up and down the coast he journeyed, saving money as he went. Whenever possible he would interview men from the West Indies and draw them out concerning the plate galleons. He would make scraggly notes of what they told him, for he was still only a poor writer. By the year 1683 he had amassed considerable information on where to go and what to do should he ever get sufficient funds to start out.

That very year he heard of another sunken treasure ship, and decided to make arrangements to start at once on a voyage for salvage. Before sailing away, he tried vainly to interest several Bostonians in his plan to recover gold from this new ship of which he had just heard, but the average sea captain of Boston scoffed at this treasure seeker and considered him merely a dreamer who would never amount to anything. They would not invest a pound in his venture, and told him bluntly what they thought of his scheme.

Anxious to prove them wrong, William Phips determined to sail without additional funds to the vicinity of what is now Key West, where the wreck had been reported. He found the wreck, recovered a little treasure with his amateurish diving gear, but eventually realized that he had failed to find the millions of which he had dreamed. His inadequate funds soon were exhausted.

Almost any other man would have returned to Boston, given up all hope of carrying out his ambitious plans for the future and stayed a sea captain for the rest of his life. But Phips decided on a gamble to risk everything, and instead of sailing back to New England, started at once in his tiny craft across the ocean to England.

Landing in Bristol, he made his first blundering attempts to get an audience with King Charles II. Rebuffed time and again, he finally met the famous Duke of Albemarle. Some time later the Duke arranged for a meeting between Charles and Phips. When Phips was brought before the King, Charles was desperately in need of funds himself, and saw in Phips' proposition a chance to rebuild his shattered finances. As a result of the conference, Charles gave the Bostonian the use of the frigate *Sally Rose,* in which he was to sail in search of sunken treasure in the West Indies. For a crew Phips raided the waterfront dens and taverns.

William Phips sailed from England early in September, 1683, stopping at Boston first, where he anchored off Little Brewster Island on October 27. Ten weeks later, after minor repairs had been made to his vessel, and diving bells and other machinery had been put aboard, the *Rose* was ready to sail.

What a ten weeks it had been, however, for both the town of Boston and William Phips! The crew had raised such terrific havoc in the taverns that Phips was placed on trial before Governor Simon Bradstreet, who decided that rather than risk further trouble, the best thing he could do for Boston was to allow Phips and his men to sail away as soon as possible.

On January 19, 1684, Phips left Boston with his boisterous

crew, bound for treasure and fame. The *Rose* arrived at Nassau and then made a visit to the location where it was believed a treasure ship had gone down. When Phips saw another ship cruising slowly in the same waters, he sailed over and flashed his King's Commission in the face of the captain of the other vessel, who promptly sailed away.

After long searching Phips had found no treasure, and finally his rough and ready crew members grew mutinous. Early one morning they started to rebel, demanding that Phips join up with them and go on a piratical cruise. When he refused, they rushed at him, but in hand-to-hand skirmish the giant sea captain from Boston felled first the ringleader and then two others with a cutlass, stopping the mutiny then and there. But the crew still had ideas of overthrowing the captain, and a short time later went ashore at an island, where they promptly notified Phips that they were planning to take over the ship. Aiming a cannon at them from the *Rose,* he informed them in no uncertain terms that he'd blow them to pieces unless they surrendered at once and came aboard. They held a hasty conference and then surrendered, going aboard one by one to be disarmed.

Deciding that two mutinies in less than a week were too much, Captain William Phips sailed at once to Jamaica, turned every man loose ashore and hired a complete new crew.

Sailing again with renewed confidence, he decided to cruise in the area near Puerto Plata, whence the fabulous plate galleons had sailed back in 1643. Following several days of fruitless endeavor just offshore, he brought his ship *Rose* into the the Puerto Plata harbor, after which he was seen in conference with an aged Spaniard, said to be the oldest man on the island of Hispaniola. Day after day passed, during which time Phips and the ancient Iberian would take long trips to another part of the island.

"You have not been searching in the right place," the aged Spaniard informed him on one of their trips. "I have been watching you with my glass, and you were too far west. Now I was on the beach right here when the vice-admiral's galleon smashed to pieces in the gale, and *there* is the location where she disappeared in the sea." The Spaniard pointed carefully with his cane at an area where silver sands could be seen, with waves breaking over them, not too far from shore.

"You send your divers down in that part of the ocean, and you'll find the treasure for which you seek," concluded the old man. They returned to Puerta Plata, where Phips paid the man well for his vital information. The Boston sea captain made plans at once to sail to the new location.

Reaching the sea area just off the silver sands, he sent his divers over the side, and they searched long and diligently. They did find the remains of an old wreck, but brought up nothing of value. Finally, with provisions low, the frigate leaking and almost all of his money spent, Phips realized that he would have to return to England, and notified his crew to prepare for departure. Stopping at Bermuda for water and supplies and a few passengers, he learned that Charles II was dead.

In August, 1685, he reached England, where one of his Bermuda passengers had him imprisoned on false charges at Tower Hill. His friends came to his support at once and had him freed. Again it was the Duke of Albemarle, himself now almost bankrupt, who interceded for Phips before King James. Albemarle seemed to have blind faith that Phips would eventually find sunken treasure. King James arranged for a new expedition to be sent out, with two vessels, the *James and Mary* and the *Henry,* to carry supplies and equipment to the location.

Reaching Puerto Plata once more, Phips sensed that the Spaniards were observing him rather carefully, and decided to stay in port aboard the *James* while sending his lieutenant, Captain Francis Rogers, to sea with the *Henry.* The men had built a small pirogue or punt which they used for rowing in and around the area, and planned to take it along when the *Henry* sailed.

On January 13, 1687, Captain Rogers, with Second Mate Covell of the *James and Mary,* and a picked crew of divers and sailors, sailed out from Puerto Plata. Nothing was heard from them until February 8. Early that morning a storm broke, and before the day had come to a close the masts and spars of the *Henry* were seen above the headlands. Soon she entered the little bay and proceeded to the pier where the other vessel was tied up.

The crew of the *James* soon realized that something extraordinary had happened. Rogers, himself a dramatic character, had planned a pleasant hoax to play on Captain Phips, and it worked. He went aboard the *James and Mary,* entered the captain's cabin, and ordered his men to stand around him while he told his story.

With a long, sorrowful face he began the narrative, and emphasized the point that they had carried out all the instructions which Phips had given. The captain's face became long, also, as the other went on with the tale. Rogers then placed the chart on the captain's table, and in doing so allowed one of the Indians an opportunity to slip under the table with a fragment of material which had actually been brought up from the bottom of the sea.

Then, in concluding his summary of events, Rogers didn't say outright that they had found nothing, but he left that impression with his leader, who felt that he should give the others more encouragement.

"We all must have plenty of patience," Phips told Rogers, as the latter rolled up his chart again. But Rogers gave a chuckle and the others in the cabin facing Phips began to smile. Mystified, Phips started to get up when his foot touched the object under the table.

"What's this?" Phips sprang to his feet. Seizing an adz which was lying nearby, he smashed at the conglomerate mass on the floor, and with the first blow the lump fell apart in all directions. Scores of golden doubloons and silver pieces of eight went spinning and sliding all over the cabin.

"Zounds!" shouted Phips, and collapsed into his chair again. A moment later he recovered himself, and announced quietly, "Thanks be to God, for we are all rich men!"

After the excitement had quieted down a little, Captain Rogers explained to his happy superior officer what had happened.

Out at the scene of the wreck, the divers had gone down almost as soon as the *Henry* had anchored. Day after day brought nothing except failure, and eventually the expedition had exhausted the area of operation. The members began to pack their gear and prepared to hoist anchor for their return to the harbor. One of the number, Second Mate William Covell, had been out in the pirogue with diver Franko, an Indian from Maine. Dr. Hans Sloane, the naturalist of the expedition, had requested the men to watch out for unusual specimens for his horticultural collection. Covell was peering down through the clear water when suddenly he sighted a beautiful sea feather far below. He signaled to Franko, who was over the side in a flash. Down, down, down through the blue water Franko sank, until finally he reached the bottom, plucked the sea feather, and then prepared to return to the surface.

But Franko took much longer than seemed necessary at the bottom of the ocean, and Covell began to wonder what he was doing. Then, with a splash and a gasp, Franko broke the surface of the sea, handed Covell the sea flower, and climbed aboard the pirogue. But his eyes were almost bursting from his head, he was so excited.

When he finally had his breath, he exclaimed, "Cannon, many cannon on bottom!" Franko went on to explain that he had seen the cannon and many more large, odd-shaped objects nearby. After a brief rest, he went over the side again, and when he returned, he had with him what appeared to be treasure, heavily encrusted in coral. Mr. Covell then signaled to the *Henry,* shouted his good news across the water to Captain Rogers, and began plans to mark the location beyond all chance of mistake.

For the next few days all the divers were busily employed

at the scene. They had actually found the wreck of the Spanish galleon, the great plate ship which had gone down there in November of 1643, and in three days they brought to the surface a vast collection of material, including pieces of eight, gold bars, broken plates, hatch bands, toggles and chests. Then the weather turned against them, and they sailed back into Puerto Plata to play their hoax on Captain Phips.

The entire expedition returned to the treasure ship with the coming of good weather, and for a month and a half each daily effort brought a new fortune from the galleon below them. But the divers began to show signs of strain, and finally the day came when the stores needed replenishing. After consultation it was agreed that they should return to England.

On May 2, 1687, the *James and Mary* and the *Henry* began their happy voyage homeward. The *James and Mary* arrived in England on June 8, and found the entire waterfront alerted. The Duke of Albemarle himself was present to board her.

"Well, Captain Phips, how went the expedition?" queried the Duke.

"Very well, Your Grace," came the answer. "The ship's hold at present contains some thirty tons of silver, gold and assorted treasure."

The Duke was amazed. "Come, now, are you serious?"

Phips dug down into his pockets and brought out handfuls of golden doubloons and silver pieces of eight.

"May—may Heaven preserve me," faltered the Duke of Albemarle as he staggered to a chair. The shock of success had been almost too much! "You have found the treasure," he kept murmuring. "You have found the treasure!" The Duke had put all his money into that expedition, and would have been penniless had Phips failed again.

Anxious to have a joke at the pleasant expense of his backers, Phips had secreted all the costly jewels which had been recovered until an opportune moment. Finally, in the presence of all those who had helped make the expedition possible, he brought out a wallet crammed with almost priceless jewels, and poured them out on the table. For the next few weeks he was the toast of all London, but then came the matter of division of the spoils. The Spanish ambassador insisted that his country should have the treasure, but the English ignored him.

Phips received what amounted to about $80,000, the equivalent of a quarter-million today, while Phips' crew and all concerned were handsomely rewarded. In all, a treasure worth $1,250,000 was recovered and the King received a substantial share of it.

The crew members enjoyed a week or so of excitement and debauchery, according to each man's individual inclination, before returning to the docks of London, but with Phips it was a different story. On June 28, 1687, the boy from Monsweag Bay, Maine, was knighted Sir William Phips by King James and was given a commission in the Royal Navy.

Further honors were to follow, but in all this time Phips had not forgotten his promise to his wife that he would build for her the "fair brick house in the Green Lane of North Boston." Sir William Phips was anxious to return to Boston and build that house, now that he had the means.

After another expedition to the scene where he had found the treasure and a moderate success there, Phips sailed for New England. This time his vessel was named, strangely enough, *Goodluck and a Boy.*

Phips landed in Boston, and was warmly welcomed by his wife. As soon as possible he began the house of his dreams, and a well-constructed building it was. His estate was located about where the corner of Salem Street and Charter Street is today. The fine brick house which he built had columns in front, two stories high, with a stately row of butternut trees leading out to his watchhouse and the stables. His gardens were so beautiful that they were the talk of all New England, while the street leading to his estate soon was called the Phips Mansion Highway.

Unfortunately, trouble began almost at once. It is true that Phips had returned to Boston a gentleman, a knight and a wealthy man, and that he wished to take his place as a prominent and distinguished American. But to Sir Edmund Andros, then Governor of New England, Phips was still an upstart. Although Phips had been named High Sheriff by King James, Andros refused to let the treasure finder take over the office on his return to Boston.

Finally, on July 6, five weeks after his arrival home, Andros reluctantly allowed Phips to assume office. But Sir William constantly became embroiled in arguments and fights while attempting to carry out his duties. He finally decided to return to England and have a conference with his London superiors.

A year later, as General Phips, he was back in America,

leading an expedition against Port Royal, Nova Scotia. Following that successful campaign, he embarked on another expedition, this time against Quebec, a campaign which ended in ignominious failure.

On January 3, 1692, Sir William Phips became Governor of the Province of Massachusetts. It was an unfortunate time to take over the rule of Massachusetts, for, among other troubles, the witch scare was at its height, political and religious strife was reaching a boiling point, and poor William had neither the tact nor the patience to control the situation.

Nevertheless, he had achieved his dream of building his fine brick house in the Green Lane of North Boston. In the years when he was wealthy, famous, and important, there were many wonderful parties and balls at his residence, where the bewigged cavaliers of the period, their glittering swords flashing against silken hosiery, gallantly escorted their beautiful dames up the grand old winding staircase. The ladies, clad in magnificent gold-embroidered brocade or damask, enjoyed to the utmost this beautifully appointed residence in North Boston, with its rich, finely-decorated rooms where beautiful tapestries hung on the walls. There Phips entertained the learned, the witty and the gay, leaders in both authority and fashion.

But an ungovernable temper became worse as he grew older, and finally there were incidents which could not be overlooked. He personally assaulted Collector of the Port Jahleel Brenton, and caned Captain Short of the frigate *Nonesuch*. The well-built Phips had an easy time subduing all opponents. One day affairs in the General Court were not going to his liking, and he personally drove all the court members into the street. Then he made a bitter enemy of Joseph Dudley.

Opponents of Phips eventually took their troubles and stories across the ocean, where they accused the Governor of mismanagement and outrageous conduct. By this time Phips had had enough of the strenuous life, and longed for peace. It came, unexpectedly, early in 1694, from across the ocean, when the English King requested his appearance before the royal throne. Phips put his house in order in Boston, and late in 1694 journeyed with his wife to England. He was never to return to America. Arriving in London, Sir William was immediately sued by Brenton and Joseph Dudley. But before the case could be settled in court, William Phips became ill, and was confined to bed. A higher Tribunal then took charge, and William Phips, one of the most remarkable men of his time, passed away on February 18, 1695.

The widow of William Phips erected a monument over his grave at the church of Saint Mary Woolnoth, attesting to the importance of the first American ever to wrest a million dollars from the sea. I quote part of the memorial below:

NEAR TO THIS PLACE IS INTERRED THE BODY OF SIR WILLIAM PHIPS, KNIGHT, WHO, IN THE YEAR 1687, BY HIS GREAT INDUSTRY DISCOVERED AMONG THE ROCKS NEAR THE BANKS OF BAHAMA, ON THE NORTH SIDE OF HISPANIOLA, A SPANISH PLATE-SHIP, WHICH HAD BEEN UNDER WATER FORTY-FOUR YEARS, OUT OF WHICH HE TOOK IN GOLD AND SILVER TO THE VALUE OF 300,000 POUNDS STERLING;

AND WITH A FIDELITY EQUAL TO HIS CONDUCT, BROUGHT
IT ALL TO LONDON WHERE IT WAS DIVIDED BETWEEN HIM-
SELF AND THE REST OF THE ADVENTURERS.

And so we come to the end of our story about the Maine
farm boy whose feat in locating and taking more than a
million dollars from the bottom of the sea makes him
among treasure finders "The Greatest of Them All." In
later life, his ungovernable temper gave him much trouble,
and perhaps there were times when he regretted becoming
wealthy. Nevertheless, do you wonder what his admonition might be to you concerning the other fourteen galleons
of the fleet which originally held treasure worth $21,000,-
000? If you are interested, I think that his advice would be
to sail away and attempt to find those other galleons, where
at least $18,000,000 still lies awaiting you at the bottom of
the West Indian sea.

CHAPTER 2

Oak Island, the Strangest Treasure Mystery

$\mathbb{M}$Y INTEREST in Oak Island's treasure began when, as a boy, I was very ill with scarlet fever. Each day I became more and more restless at my enforced inactivity. In my mother's room, where the doctor had confined me, was a large, under-the-eaves closet, which went far back under the roof. There were stored hundreds of copies of the *Youth's Companion, Outlook, Saint Nicholas, Atlantic Monthly* and a few *Collier's,* some dating back to the 1890's. The magazines had been saved for just such an occasion as my illness, and I soon became fascinated by their contents. Every day I pored over them and each one offered me a new adventure in reading. But there was one story I shall never forget. It was in *Collier's*—a true story of a treasure buried on Oak Island, off the coast of Nova Scotia.

When I recovered, the doctor gave orders to burn all the magazines I had handled. The Oak Island treasure tale was thrown into the fire with the others, but I remembered the date of the story's publication, 1905.

One day in 1939 I was reading a *Popular Science* magazine and again I came across a story about Oak Island and its undiscovered treasure. My old interest was revived. The following Saturday I went to the Boston Public Library and searched through the 1905 issues of *Collier's* until I found the article on Oak Island. From that moment on, I saved every bit of information I could spot about the island and finally was able to piece together its strange history.

Oak Island lies in Mahone Bay, Nova Scotia, about thirty miles to the south of Halifax. Approximately two and a half miles long and a mile wide, it is the ideal location for buried treasure. Protected from the ocean by the Tancook Islands at the entrance to Mahone Bay, it is far enough offshore to be completely secluded.

Certain other facts about the island can be easily proved. The first is that, at some time in the eighteenth century and perhaps earlier, a group of people dug a pit there about twelve feet in diameter and more than one hundred feet in depth. The second fact is that the pit was connected underground with the ocean, 460 feet away, as a safeguard against those who might disturb the treasure. The third is that at the bottom of the pit were placed large wooden containers of metal or coins. The fourth item is really an assumption, rather than a proved fact. It is that the metal or coins must have been of considerable number or value, because of the extensive efforts made to conceal the treasure from others.

Few residents of the vicinity knew anything of Oak Island's mysteries until the year 1795. In the fall of that year three boys from Chester, on the mainland—Daniel McInnis, Anthony Vaughn and Jack Smith—went hunting on the deserted island. About 400 feet from the shore, they came upon a tall oak tree with a branch worn off in such a way as to indicate that a heavy hoist or cable had been used there. The three boys were strangely excited by their discovery, for, as far as was locally known, there had never been activity of any sort on the island.

Examining the ground in the vicinity of the tree, the boys noticed a slight depression, about twelve feet in diameter, directly under the worn-off limb. They studied the land nearby but found no other clues. They finally decided to return home but to come back again as soon as possible. Quite probably not one of the trio slept much that night, each thinking of what might be buried on Oak Island and what he could do with his share of the treasure, if treasure it proved to be.

Early the next day the boys returned to the island, armed with picks and shovels. As they began to dig, they noticed that the earth was softer within the slightly sunken twelve-foot-wide area than outside, confirming their belief that the ground had been previously shoveled. They also detected gashes that might have been made by a pick at the outside rim of the space as they dug deeper and deeper. When they had gone down ten feet, they hit something solid—a wooden plank which they were confident served as a protection for a treasure chest. But the obstruction was merely a platform of logs. When they removed it, they found nothing but earth below. This was such a bitter disappointment that the boys decided to go home. Discouraged and weary, they paddled back to the mainland.

But sleep soothes tired backs and weary bodies, and the fascination of possible buried treasure still held them. At the next opportunity they again went out to the island. When they had dug down twenty feet more, they struck another platform. This time their hopes were tempered by experience so they were not too desperately disappointed when again they found nothing but earth under the platform.

Week after week, month after month, the boys went out to the island whenever they could. Eventually the project became too much for them; they needed special equipment and engineers to advise them. While they were planning to arrange for help, snowstorms forced them to discontinue their efforts for the winter.

Back in Chester, the three boys began talking about their activities on Oak Island. An old woman with whom they talked revealed a strange story that her own grandmother had related years before. In 1720 the people of the mainland had observed peculiar lights burning on Oak Island at night. Boatmen curious enough to cruise in the vicinity had seen the outlines of men believed to be pirates silhouetted against giant bonfires. Two fishermen who went to Oak Island to investigate did not return and were never heard from again. Finally the pirates, if such they were, disappeared from Mahone Bay, and the area settled down to quietness and peace. But the women of Chester whose men had vanished never forgot the days when the pirates were active at Oak Island.

A feeling of terror toward the island had persisted ever since the 1720's and the three boys found it impossible to get a sponsor for their project. The years passed and no further attempts were made to locate the treasure, if treasure there was. The boys grew to manhood and married.

Dan McInnis and Jack Smith settled on Oak Island itself, but Anthony Vaughn moved to a house on the mainland. According to legend, Jack Smith's wife did not want their first baby to be born on Oak Island because of its mysterious history. The couple traveled to Truro, Nova Scotia, and stayed at the home of a Dr. John Lynds. When the mother and baby returned to Oak Island, Dr. Lynds came along with them. He had been bitten badly by the treasure bug and wished to see the island for himself. When he was offered payment for his services he is said to have refused and suggested that his fee should consist of one share of a treasure-seeking company. In this strange manner the first Oak Island treasure company came into being.

Dr. Lynds soon made an exhaustive study of the place where the pit had been dug. Examining the tree, he found marks and figures on its trunk, and noticed that the branch which had been worn off was the largest of all the branches, and projected directly out over the center of the pit itself. Inspecting the planking, Dr. Lynds found that the ends of the logs had been embedded in the sides of the pit to prevent a sinking at the surface, causing a depression which might be detected and eventually cause whatever was buried in the pit to be discovered. Dr. Lynds climbed down into the hole and scraped away at the final tier of logs, thirty feet below the surface, where the boys had ceased their labors. Later he examined a strange ringbolt attached to one of the beach boulders.

Dr. Lynds then traveled to Halifax, where he interested several prominent men in forming a company. Before long equipment began arriving on the island.

Down, down and down the diggers went. At forty feet, fifty feet and sixty feet platforms were reached and passed. At seventy and eighty feet there were platforms containing a strange, fiberlike material placed next to charcoal. A substance resembling putty was found at another tier. The mystery grew stranger and stranger, but when the ninety-foot mark was reached, the greatest mystery of all awaited the diggers. It was a round, flat stone, about three feet high and sixteen inches wide. On the face of the stone curious characters had been cut:

$$\nabla \dot{\times} \, \emptyset \triangle \swarrow \nabla :: \triangle \; \top : \mathsf{C} \dot{\times} \square \; \triangle \square \dot{\times}$$

$$\rightthreetimes \therefore \mathsf{C} \mathsf{C} \therefore \times \times \; \ominus \dot{\times} + \swarrow \mathbb{I} \odot \; \cdot \emptyset \colon \; \dagger \dagger \emptyset \therefore \colon \mathbb{I}$$

Reverend A. T. Kempton of Cambridge, Massachusetts, believes that an old Irish schoolmaster worked out the code and translated the inscription to read, letter for letter, as follows:

> FORTY FEET BELOW TWO
> MILLION POUNDS ARE BURIED

However, it is only fair to state that there are many who claim that the above inscription was not the one found on the stone.

One Saturday evening shortly after the stone had been found, the men reached a depth of ninety-five feet. An iron bar was shoved down through the bottom of the pit and at three feet another wooden platform was struck. The men then stopped work for the weekend. When they returned Monday morning the shaft was filled with water to within thirty-five feet of the surface! The men began to bail it out, working day and night, but in spite of their efforts, the water remained at the same level in the pit. Finally, in desperation, they decided to sink another shaft, and drain the water into the new shaft.

Work was started at once, and in a reasonably short time the shaft had reached 110 feet! Then a tunnel was driven horizontally across to the money pit. Suddenly water burst in and flooded the new tunnel as well. This so discouraged the operators, whose funds were by now exhausted, that they abandoned their activities and returned to the mainland.

Perhaps the continuous flood of the shaft was caused by the removal of the strange, flat stone. In order to defeat anyone who persevered in looking for the treasure to the extent of digging ninety feet underground, the stone may have been placed as a key to unlock the drains from the ocean.

The years went by and grass covered the entrance to both pits at Oak Island. It was not until the California Gold Rush of 1849 that enough enthusiasm was found to float another treasure-hunting organization. Dr. Lynds and Anthony Vaughn of the original company were still alive and gave the manager of the new project much valuable information. Both expressed their confidence that the treasure was still at the bottom of the money pit.

Digging began soon afterwards, and the eighty-six-foot mark was attained before water again came pouring in. Bailing casks were sent down, but no further progress could be made. Primitive boring apparatus of the type used by coal miners was then taken out to Oak Island and placed in charge of Mr. J. B. McCully of Truro. He ordered a platform built about thirty feet down in the money pit, just above the reach of the water. The boring began with a pod auger. For the purpose of accuracy, I now quote directly from J. B. McCully's statement:

The platform was struck at ninety-eight feet, just as the diggers found it when sounding with the iron bar. After going through the platform which was five inches thick, and proved to be of spruce, the auger dropped twelve inches and then went through four inches of oak, then through twenty-two inches of metal in pieces, but the auger failed to bring up anything in the nature of treasure except three links resembling the links of a watch chain. The auger then went through eight inches of oak, which was thought to be the bottom of the first box and top of the next, then twenty-two inches of metal, the same as before, and four inches of oak and six inches of spruce, then into clay seven feet without striking anything else.

In boring a second hole the platform was struck as before at ninety-eight feet; passing through this, the auger fell about eighteen inches and came in contact with (as supposed) the side of a cask. The auger revolving close to the side of the cask gave a jerky and irregular motion. On withdrawing the auger several splinters of oak, such as might come from an oak stave, and a small quantity of a brown, fibrous substance, closely resembling the husk of a cocoanut, were brought up. The difference between the upper and lower platforms was six feet.

The foreman in charge of the drilling was one John Pitblado. His instructions were to remove the drill at periodic intervals and scrape off the material brought up so that it could be examined under a microscope. One of the men present at the boring operations was Mr. John Gamel, a prominent citizen of Upper Stewiacke, Nova Scotia. He was a large stockholder in the new company and was allowed to stand fairly close to the auger as it operated. Neither his honesty nor his truthfulness can be questioned.

Late one particular day, when he thought no one was watching him, Pitblado slowly brought the drill out of the pit. Then he took something from the auger, washed it, examined it carefully, and slid it into his pocket, but not before the alert eye of Gamel saw him.

"What have you there, Pitblado? Don't you think we should all see it?"

"Why, yes, you'll all get a chance at our next director's conference," replied Pitblado, and refused to reveal what it was he had hurriedly concealed in his pocket. That night Pitblado disappeared from the island and never returned. No one ever learned what it was that he had removed from the auger, for he was killed the following month in a gold mine accident.

Soon after the disappearance of Pitblado, the company

stopped operations for the year, and it was not until the summer of 1850 that work was resumed. At that time a new shaft was sent down on the western side of the original money pit, ten feet away. Mr. A. A. Tupper, also of Upper Stewiacke, has left us an account of the operations.

A tunnel was driven from the bottom in the direction of the "Money Pit." Just before reaching the "Money Pit" the water burst in, the workers fled for their lives, and in twenty minutes there was forty-five feet of water in the new shaft. The sole object in view in sinking this shaft was to increase the bailing facilities, for which purpose preparations had been made, and bailing was resumed in both the new and old shafts, each being equipped with two 2-horse gins. Work was carried on night and day for about a week, but all in vain, the only difference being that with the doubled appliances, the water could be kept at a lower level.

Shortly afterwards, it was discovered that the water in the pit was salt and must have poured in from the ocean. Since the water could not enter the money pit through a narrow channel without submerging the original diggers of the pit, an underground tunnel must have been built by those who had constructed it in the first place. A search was made around the entire island for traces of an artificial entrance somewhere along the shore. Smith's Cove was located near the eastern point of Oak Island, about 460 feet from the entrance to the money pit, and a careful examination of the cove indicated that construction work had been carried on there. A cofferdam was hastily erected at the low tide mark so that the entrance for the water which flooded the pit could be located.

The first signs of a man-made entrance were masses of a brown fiber, two inches in thickness, which were discovered under the sand and gravel on the beach. It appeared to be the same fiber which had been found in the money pit. The fiber extended 145 feet along the shore, from a little above low water to the high water mark. Four or five inches of eelgrass were found below the fibrous material, and under the eelgrass the workmen located a compact mass of beach rocks, completely free from either sand or gravel.

Now the diggers discovered an amazingly complex drainwork construction under the beach rock. Five drains had been built by laying parallel lines of rocks eight inches apart and covering them with flat stones. The drains resembled five fingers stretched out from a hand, converging at a common center on the inner or high tide side of the excavation. When the tide rose, water spilled over the top of the cofferdam and the men were forced to discontinue their examination of the ingenious drainage system.

Another shaft was sunk on the southern side of the money pit, to a depth of 118 feet—the greatest yet attained—and from here a tunnel was driven toward the bottom of the money pit. Hopes were high for success. But during lunch hour one day a tremendous crash was heard, and one of the workmen, Publicover by name, came running from the tunnel.

"I got out just in time!" he shouted.

The diggers realized that the bottom of the money pit had fallen into the new tunnel. It was fortunate for them that they had not been working there at the time. The 118-

foot shaft rapidly filled with water. Later it was discovered that twelve feet of mud had been driven into the new shaft by the accident. With funds exhausted, the new company retired from the island defeated.

As far as we know, the next effort to locate the treasure at Oak Island did not begin until 1863, when a powerful engine and pump were brought over to the island and the water in the 118-foot shaft was kept below the 100-foot level. But the men working in the shaft felt that it was in danger of caving in. An expert engineer was called in to examine the project. He found that the workmen's fears were well-grounded. The shaft was in imminent danger of collapse. The pump was taken out and the shaft abandoned.

In Halifax, another company was soon formed with great enthusiasm. This group contracted with those in control to clean out the old money pit and share in whatever treasure might be found. Their first step was to sink a new shaft, but this failed to stop the flow of water. Then they sank several tunnels to intercept the horizontal tunnel from Smith's Cove beach. In this they failed completely, abandoned their efforts and returned to Halifax. But the pits they had dug caused considerable trouble thereafter to other companies seeking the treasure.

Years later a farmer was plowing on the island with his oxen some distance from the money pit when suddenly, without warning, the oxen went down in a hole. The ground had given way, and the farmer barely saved himself by leaping to one side. The hole that formed was six or eight feet wide and about fifteen feet deep. Without question, it was part of the air shaft which led down to the horizontal tunnel from Smith's Cove.

In the year 1893 a young man named Frederick L. Blair was bitten by the Oak Island treasure bug, as scores of others had been since 1795. But this young man was different. He was extraordinarily intelligent, had substantial funds to invest, and was eager and willing to push the project to completion. A single failure was not going to discourage him. He was seventeen years old when he first invested money in the project.

The new organization, formed in 1893 as the Oak Island Treasure Company, did not plan too well in the beginning, according to Mr. Blair. The money pit was opened and widened and a deep shaft started. At 111 feet a horizontal tunnel was found, two and a half feet wide, through which sea water flowed with great force. This tunnel was square in shape, and before the water stopped progress, a chip of wood, a bird's bone, and pieces of bark were discovered in it. These three objects convinced the treasure seekers that there had been human activity far below the surface of the earth. But the ocean's force gradually overcame the workers and the money pit filled up with sea water again.

The group decided to stop the flow near its source. They drilled five suitably spaced holes fifty feet inland from Smith's Cove and set off dynamite at the base of each hole. Hole number three was made where they believed the horizontal tunnel had been placed. One hundred and sixty pounds of dynamite failed to bring water to the surface, although in each of the other holes water went high in the air after each blast. Also it was noted that the blast from number three hole caused the water in the money pit to seethe and foam for some time afterwards, and the water there rose and fell with the tide.

Up to this time, no one dreamed that the treasure might be below 118 feet, but when the workmen in the money pit found loose debris and soil there, they continued drilling to a greater depth.

William Chappell and T. Perley Putnam were among those who drilled for the treasure during 1897. Chappell found that in the four drill holes made that year blue clay was encountered 130 feet down, and again found at 160 feet. One drill struck wood at 122 feet and later at 126 feet. Iron was reached at 126 feet and cement at 151 feet in another hole. Chappell believed that metal in bars and coin or metal in small pieces was struck and passed in this particular hole.

One small, fibrous ball, about the size of a grain of rice, with fuzz or short hair on the surface, was brought up by the drill. After careful work, the substance was flattened out and proved to be a small piece of parchment, with the letters *ui, vi,* or *wi* written on it in black ink.

Despite this important discovery, the company was forced to give up its efforts at the island because the funds had been exhausted. In 1898, however, more funds were made available by Mr. Blair, and additional holes were sunk around the money pit, in the vain hope that the water in the pit could be drained off. The plan proved impossible, as have several other plans since that time. The results have always been the same, and to this day no one *knows* what is buried there.

In April, 1947, I determined to visit Oak Island, and flew up there with Major Paul Dudley in his amphibian plane. As we flew up the coast I told Paul the dramatic history of the island.

Finally, we sighted the waters of Mahone Bay. Cruising along at seven hundred feet, we found the great number of islands quite confusing, but finally located the town of Chester, and flew back over the lighthouse on Quaker Island. Then not too far away, we recognized the fabled isle of legend and mystery: Oak Island.

We landed at Oak Island the next day, but before doing so we visited Amherst, Nova Scotia, to talk with Frederick L. Blair, whose interest in the island began many years ago. He told us that he has spent a lifetime attempting to solve the mystery of Oak Island. He was kindly and thoughtful, and his brown eyes, white hair and patient manner gave me the feeling that whatever he might say would prove to be true.

The minutes flew by as we talked. I asked him how he originally became interested in Oak Island. He explained that when a boy, he was fascinated by stories which Mr. Jefferson W. McDonald had told him about the island, and of McDonald's adventures there. McDonald had worked there in the 1860's and was present when the money pit collapsed. I asked Mr. Blair what probably happened to the treasure which was contacted by the drill in 1849.

"I wish I could answer that question," replied Mr. Blair. "The best guess we can make is that when the 118-foot shaft was sunk under the money pit at an angle and the whole shaft collapsed, it brought down the treasure itself. The momentum then carried the treasure down through another weakly-braced partition until it finally lodged some 150 feet below the surface."

Mr. Blair also told me about Publicover's escape at the time of the money pit's collapse. As Publicover, the last man to escape, ran for safety, he picked up a small yellow keg cover which had dropped through a crevice. A moment later he appeared at the entrance to the shaft, just as the whole tunnel collapsed behind him with a loud crash. The keg cover had fallen down through from the treasure room itself.

Finally we left Mr. Blair and returned to the Amherst airport, where H. Borden Pye offered to go with us to Oak Island. An hour later we circled Oak Island, landed near a sandy beach suitable for the plane, and taxied in toward shore.

When the water shallowed off I opened the forward hatch door, watching carefully for underwater obstructions. We grounded the plane in eighteen inches of water, and I pulled off my shoes and socks, rolled up my trousers and waded ashore. At last I had reached Oak Island!

We hiked around the island, following a well-defined path which led up to the money pit, passing huge mounds of earth, the product of a century and a half of digging. Reaching the fenced-in area where the original money pit stood, I leaped over the fence and ran toward the shaft. Heavy timbers led down into the ground, and I couldn't resist the urge to descend into the money pit. Down and down I went, testing each beam to see if it was strong enough to bear my weight. Five minutes later I was down as far as I dared go, probably forty feet below the surface. Looking up, I could see only a small square of light far above me. The air was damp from rotting timbers. In the dim light I could discern below me refuse and debris of all sorts, on top of which reposed a no-trespassing sign.

As I clung there two-thirds of the way down the pit, I had the sensation that I was in a series of elevator shafts similar to those in a modern building. The frame work descended on either side of me in both directions. I realized that the entire area was honeycombed with adjacent shafts. Finally I climbed out into the sunlight.

Some distance from the top of the pit I noticed a small boulder, about eighteen inches high. On it was an inscription that read, IN MEMORY OF CAPT. KID, 1701. It had been placed there some years ago by a group of treasure hunters. They had named the location Camp Kidd, as a tribute to the famous privateer, who many mistakenly believe was a pirate.

We were also interested in examining the beach where the cofferdam can still be seen. We walked over to Smith's Beach. The tide was still low, and before us were the old half-moon remains of the ancient cofferdam. Here workmen of another day had constructed their water tunnel to the treasure, the tunnel which has prevented so many expeditions from bringing the great treasure to the surface.

But in the west the sun was sinking dangerously low, and we returned to our plane and soon were airborne over Oak Island. I took my final pictures, and then we flew up the coast to Dartmouth, where we spent the night.

Perhaps some day the mystery of Oak Island and its treasure will be solved. There are so many theories and explanations regarding the treasure, yet the true story may not be similar to any of them. I personally like to think that it is an immense hoard brought to Oak Island from a South American country at a time when invaders threatened that part of the world. Frederick Blair, whose lifetime of research and endeavor makes his opinion a valued one, told me that the knowledge he has obtained in respect to Oak Island makes him a firm believer in the existence of buried treasure there. He believes that some day some one will recover it, and then, at long last, he will know the answer to one of the world's greatest mysteries: WHO BURIED WHAT AT OAK ISLAND?

CHAPTER 3

The Pirate Ship Whidah's Baffling Hoard

A PIRATE ship which has attracted great attention down through the years is the old three-masted galleon *Whidah*, whose hulk is still to be seen at times off Cape Cod's shores at Wellfleet, Massachusetts. Buccaneer Captain Samuel Bellamy was wrecked at Wellfleet aboard the *Whidah* on April 26, 1717, and he and 143 of his crew drowned in the mighty surf there. Only two men were saved.

Although the *Whidah* can still be visited in comparatively shallow water not too far off the beach at Wellfleet, it is only fair to state that great confusion exists, even among the natives, as to which vessel of several wrecked in that area is actually the *Whidah*.

Whenever I am in the vicinity, no matter how busy I happen to be, whether hiking along the beach or flying above it, I always spare a few moments to look for the old pirate ship. As late as the War between the States the iron caboose of the *Whidah* showed above water at low tide, and in 1923 John Howard Nickerson saw the remains of the *Whidah* just out of water at extreme low tide.

Without possible question, the present-day value of the gold and silver still believed to be aboard the *Whidah* is no less than half a million dollars.

The story of Bellamy and the *Whidah* is an unusual one. Captain Samuel Bellamy, who is believed to have come originally from the West Indies, was notorious up and down this coast as a bloodthirsty buccaneer, filibusterer and pirate. He first appears in the records when he joined up with Paulsgrave Williams of Nantucket, later a resident of Newport, Rhode Island. Bellamy's connection with piracy appears to have started innocently enough. Early in 1716 he and Williams learned of the existence of a Spanish galleon wreck in the West Indies, just as William Phips gained similar information years before. Phips had found his treasure, however, as I relate elsewhere in this book.

Unfortunately, the Bellamy expedition failed. After sailing to the wreck, Bellamy sent down divers to explore the bottom of the sea. The weeks went by, their provisions ran out, and still nothing of value was recovered. Finally, they were forced to stop their efforts and give up in despair, for they had found nothing, not a single bag of gold or silver!

Terribly discouraged, the two leaders were embarrassed at the thought of returning penniless to New England, for they had predicted that they would come back rich men. Another course of activity was then discussed, piracy on the high seas. Bellamy and Williams agreed that they would "go on the account," the popular expression for piracy in those days.

Meeting two well-established pirates shortly afterwards, Captain Benjamin Thornigold and Captain Louis Lebous, Bellamy and Williams agreed to pool resources with the veterans. Thornigold became captain of one of the two sloops available, taking seventy men with him, and Bellamy assumed command of the other sloop, also having a crew of seventy. For the next few months they went on a pirating cruise in which many vessels were encountered and captured. The fighting, however, was so bitter that no less than twenty-four of the pirates were killed.

After a few weeks of successful marauding enterprises, during which many unusual seizures were made, a dispute arose when Captain Thornigold refused to plunder any more English vessels. This attitude finally led to a break between the pirates, with Samuel Bellamy retaining a majority of the men, ninety in number, leaving Thornigold to sail away in a prize sloop with only twenty-six cutthroats aboard. Captain Lebous joined forces with Bellamy and together they sailed the high seas, spreading to the breeze a large black flag with a skull and cross bones. After several important captures, on December sixteenth, they were sailing off the island of Blanco, in the West Indies, when they fell in with a Bristol ship, the *Saint Michael,* bound for Jamaica with provisions. Capturing the ship and crew without too much trouble, they brought it into Blanco harbor.

Men from the *Saint Michael* figure prominently in the subsequent career of the famous pirate.

While at Blanco, Bellamy's men forced into pirate membership four of the crew of the captured vessel, including Thomas Davis, a Welshman. When Davis was informed of the pirates' intention to force him to join them, he cried out in despair that he was undone. Seeing that Davis was having a hard time with the pirates, Captain Williams of the *Saint Michael* tried to intercede for him. Finally Captain Bellamy agreed that Davis could be put on the next vessel that was taken.

On January 9, 1717, Davis was placed with fourteen other forced men aboard the *Sultana,* which had been made into a galley after its capture a short time before. The pirate fleet sailed for Testagos, where they put the ships in order, after which they parted company with Captain Lebous. Reaching Saint Croix, they blew up a French pirate ship.

Toward the end of the month of February, 1717, a fine galley, the *Whidah,* was sighted making her way through the Windward Passage, between Cuba and Porto Rico, bound for London from Jamaica. Having just completed a successful trading voyage along the Guinea coast, the *Whidah* was loaded with a rich cargo of indigo, Jesuit's bark, elephant's teeth, gold dust, sugar and other commodities. Captain Lawrence Prince was in command of the *Whidah,* and his action on being challenged by the pirates stamps him as an extremely timid man.

Three long days and nights the pirates pursued the *Whidah,* finally maneuvering close enough at the end of the third day to fire a shot at the galley. To Bellamy's amazement, the *Whidah* promptly hauled down her flag in surrender, offering no resistance of any kind. The pirate leader chose a prize crew to go aboard the galley, and the three vessels then sailed for the Bahama Islands. Here Bellamy transferred several of his guns to the *Whidah,* and told Captain Prince he could sail for home on the *Sultana,* loading aboard her any of the goods not desired by the pirates. Bellamy gave the captain twenty pounds in silver and gold as a farewell token of friendship, and then Captain Prince sailed the *Sultana* over the horizon to England.

Thomas Davis, the forced man who had been promised his freedom, requested permission to sail with Prince before he started, but was turned down. When Captain Bellamy agreed to leave it up to the pirate crew, the men voted against Davis' leaving them, as they said Davis was a carpenter and was badly needed aboard. "Blast him," said the company, "rather than let him go he should be shot or whipped to death at the mast."

Incidentally, the spelling of the name of the pirate craft is controversial. George Francis Dow and John Henry Edmonds, in their masterly work on New England pirates, use the spelling *Whidaw,* while Sidney Perley, historian of Salem, chooses *Whidah.* In the booklet issued after the execution of the six pirates, the spelling *Whido* is preferred, but the most fantastic possibility was suggested some years ago —that the *Whidah* actually was the *Quedah,* a vessel captured by Captain Kidd himself. Many other spellings are known. We probably never shall be certain of the real spelling.

About twenty thousand pounds in money had been taken

in the *Whidah's* capture, and this rich prize was stored between decks without a guard. As there were 180 men aboard, the money was divided into 180 bags, each weighing fifty pounds.

Five more ships were encountered. Bellamy's buccaneers stopped an English vessel, laden with sugar and indigo, looted it, and allowed the craft to proceed. Then two Scottish ships were taken and, the next day, a vessel from Bristol, England, a town from which many of the pirates hailed. Finally, they sighted the last of the five ships, a craft from Scotland, loaded with rum and sugar, but leaking badly; in fact, it was in such deplorable condition that when a prize crew sent aboard refused to continue the journey, a vote was taken to abandon her. A scow captured previously was now brought alongside, so that the crew could be transferred before they scuttled the leaking rum ship.

During the afternoon, when the sea marauders were sending the Scottish rum ship to the bottom, flashes of lightning could be seen in the distance, and before long a severe thunderstorm had descended upon the pirate fleet. Captain Bellamy ordered his men to take in all small canvas and Captain Paulsgrave Williams, on the other ship, double-reefed his main sail. The storm was so violent that in one fearful gust of wind the *Whidah* nearly capsized, and it was only by expert seamanship that she was saved. The wind was northwest, driving the pirate fleet away from the American coast. Great, towering waves, with white, dangerous crests, were encountered everywhere, and the fearful wind forced Bellamy to scud along with only the goose-wings of the foresail set. As night came on, the tempest increased in fury. To quote from a contemporary account in Johnson's *History of the Pirates,* the storm in its fearful intensity

"obliged the Whidaw to bring her yards aportland, and all they could do with Tackles to the Goose Neck of the Tiler, four Men in the Gun Room, and two at the Wheel, was to keep her Head to the Sea, for had she once broach'd to, they must infallibly have founder'd. The Heavens, in the mean while, were covered with Sheets of Lightning, which the Sea by the Agitation of the saline Particles seem'd to imitate; the Darkness of the Night was such, as the Scripture says, as might be felt; the terrible hollow roarings of the Winds, cou'd be only equalled by the repeated, I may say, incessant Claps of Thunder. . . .

The vessels sailed the night through under bare poles, the main mast of the *Whidah* was cut down after being sprung in the step, and the mizzen mast went by the board. "These misfortunes," says Johnson, "made the Ship ring with Blasphemy," which was increased when the *Whidah* was found to be leaking badly. The sloop was also in a weakened condition. The storm continued for four days and three nights before it abated. Then the wind, which had been shifting all around the compass, turned to north north-east, and diminished in intensity, so the pirates were allowed a breathing spell from the elements.

But the *Whidah* continued to leak severely. The lee pump had to be manned continually, day and night, in order to keep the water at a constant level. The carpenter finally crawled up in the bows to find the leak. After considerable effort he located the break, repaired it, and clambered back from the bows. The pirates could now rest from their pumping labors. It was agreed that a run to Ocracoke Inlet, off the coast of Carolina, should be attempted, but the pirates encountered a southerly wind that made them change their plans completely. They decided instead to try to reach the waters of Southern New England, where they could visit friends in Rhode Island. One sunny day, as these wastrels of the deep were relaxing on board, the lookout spotted a sloop in the distance. Quickly overtaking her, they found that the sloop was from Boston and commanded by a Rhode Island man named Beer. After a short skirmish Captain Beer surrendered. The pirates made fast work of the task of plundering his vessel. Although both Captain Bellamy and Paulsgrave Williams were in favor of allowing Beer to keep his sloop, the others out-voted them and the vessel was sent to the bottom. Johnson tells us of Captain Bellamy's conversation with Beer.

Captain Bellamy did his best to make Beer join his pirate band, but Beer declined the doubtful compliment. The buc-caneers then put Beer in a small boat and landed him at Block Island. There he obtained passage to Rhode Island, reaching his Newport home on the first of May, when he told his astonished friends of the misfortunes which he had suffered.

We now approach the time of the dramatic shipwreck of the *Whidah* on the white sands of the great beach at Cape Cod. Early on Friday morning, April 26, the pirate ships were about halfway between Nantucket Shoals and the George's Banks, sailing along at a steady clip, when sud-denly the lookout sighted a vessel, which soon was over-taken and captured. It proved to be the wine pinky, *Mary Ann,* from Dublin, Ireland, in command of Captain Andrew Crumpstey, and bound for New York. Her entire cargo was Madeira wine. Captain Crumpstey and five of his crew were ordered aboard the *Whidah,* and seven armed men took over the pinky.

When news of the type of cargo aboard the *Mary Ann* became known, a small boat was sent across to bring back some wine, and the craft returned to the *Whidah* with several dozen bottles of the beverage. Orders were given to steer a course northwest by north, but before long another vessel hove into sight. This was a Virginia sloop, which was promptly captured and manned by the pirates. The buccaneer fleet now consisted of four vessels. As evening approached, they all put out lights astern and made sail, keeping together.

Aboard the wine pinky, *Mary Ann,* the pirates lost no time in getting gloriously drunk, each taking a turn at the wheel while the others went below to indulge. As the night passed, the pinky was discovered to be leaking badly, and several of the pirates were forced to man the pumps. To make matters more serious, a storm from the east, which had been threatening for some time, suddenly broke loose in all its fury, and the rain came down so hard that the ships completely lost touch with each other in the gale.

It was shortly after this that the buccaneers aboard the pinky heard that most-feared of all sounds at sea—breakers on a lee shore. All hands rushed to trim head sail but it was too late. Before any steps could be taken to prevent it, the *Mary Ann* hit heavily on a sandy shore. It was Cape Cod where the pirate craft struck, at a point just opposite Sluttsbush, back of Stage Harbor. The location is now identified with Orleans, Massachusetts. Pirate Thomas Baker, the commander of the pinky, ordered the masts cut away, and the vessel soon drove up on the beach.

Some of the pirates, realizing that either the sea or the people of Massachusetts would soon have them, asked Captain Baker to read out loud from a prayer book. Baker, also believing that the situation was one of extreme gravity, took them down in the hold, where he read from the book of common prayer for a full hour. Daylight came, however, without the pinky's breaking up, and at low tide the men all jumped down to a dry beach. They found themselves on Pochet Island, now a part of the Orleans mainland.

In need of sustenance, they ate sweetmeats which had washed ashore in a chest, and drank some more wine from part of the cargo which had come up on the beach. Looking oceanward, the unhappy buccaneers noticed the masts and spars of the snow and the sloop, which had both ridden out the storm. The great flagship *Whidah* could not be seen anywhere, and the seven men rightfully concluded that Bellamy had met disaster.

At ten o'clock that morning, John Cole and another man who had seen the wreck from the mainland paddled out to the island by canoe, and took all seven of the pirates ashore to Cole's home. The pirates later decided to try to escape to Rhode Island, where in those days they had many friends, and asked Cole how to reach that destination.

The forced men then started trouble for the pirates. Mackconachy, the cook aboard the pinky, bravely denounced the seven pirates for what they were while they were still at Cole's home. As soon as possible, Cole sent a messenger to Justice Joseph Doane of Eastham. This good man told his deputy sheriff to organize a posse at once. Meanwhile, the pirates had reached the tavern at Eastham, where they were indulging in refreshments. A short time later, in the midst of their repast, the posse crashed in on them from all sides and made the buccaneers surrender. Their journey continued in the direction of Rhode Island, it is true, but it came to a sudden stop at the Barnstable jail, where the pirates were imprisoned.

The buccaneers aboard the *Whidah* fared no better. The old Wellfleet Life Saving Station, about twelve miles north of Orleans, is the nearest modern day marker by which we can identify the present location of the pirate wreck. The *Whidah* was pushed toward the breakers near this place, finally coming to grief about two miles south of the Wellfleet Life Saving Station site. Whether the *Whidah* was caught in the trough of the sea or whether she split in two cannot be ascertained. Although Captain Bellamy attempted to anchor off the breakers, the sea was so boisterous that the pirates cut the cable and tried to work their way off shore, but the great ship soon struck heavily on the bar, probably capsizing shortly afterwards. Of the 146 men aboard the *Whidah* all except two perished beneath the waves. Thus death by drowning off the Cape Cod beach was the end of the notorious Captain Samuel Bellamy, a typical pirate of colonial times.

One of the two men who successfully accomplished the swim ashore in the great combers was Thomas Davis, who had been forced from the *Saint Michael* the preceding December. The other survivor was John Julian, a Cape Cod

Airplane view of Oak Island, Nova Scotia, where treasure is still being sought. (Planking is location for money pit.)

Collection of pirate gold and silver owned by a resident of Belmont, Massachusetts, who does not wish his name revealed.

The author with metal detector at Cape Cod.

John Light, who in 1949 was New England's youngest diver at 16, is shown in the midst of his diving regalia. Some day he hopes to bring up pirate treasure.

Wallace Wyman, of Winthrop, who lived near pirate treasure for many years and never found it. The ship's quarterboard is from a wreck at Deer Island.

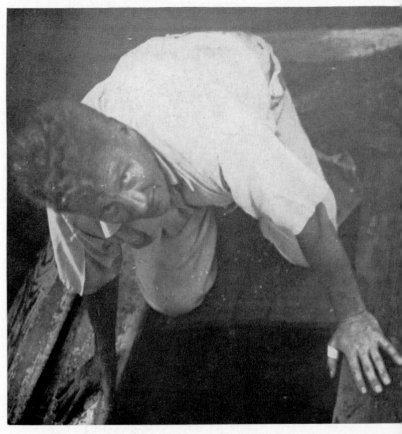

The author about to descend into cellar of ruined house at Middle Brewster.

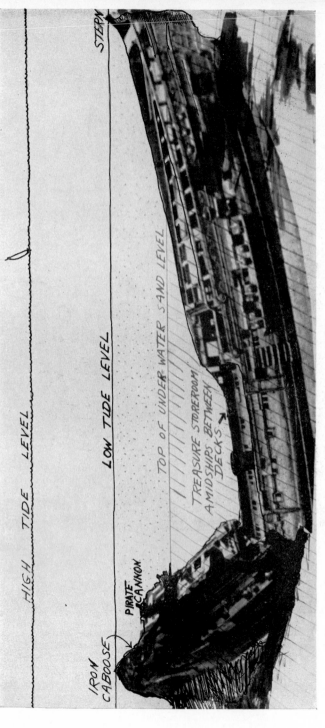

Cross-sectional sketch of present position of pirate ship *Whidah* deep in under-water sand off Wellfleet.

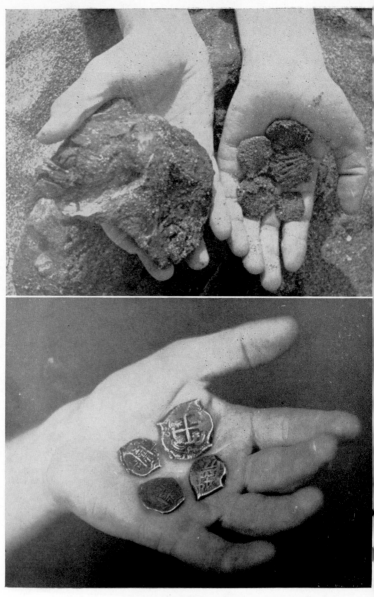

(*Above*) Holding fragments which later proved to be pieces of four and pieces of eight.

(*Below*) Cleaned fragments of coins.

Indian, who was thrown ashore by the sea almost at his own doorstep.

A controversy raged a few months later as to how the prisoners aboard the *Whidah* met their death. Preaching from the pulpit one Sunday morning, Cotton Mather expressed his belief that the pirates had murdered all of the sixteen prisoners, including Captain Crumpstey, just before their own death, but no testimony agrees with him. Anyone who has seen dead bodies after the battering of a few hours in a heavy surf can understand why Mather believed the prisoners had been murdered, but as Davis, the only white survivor, did not mention this possibility it is safe to think that all aboard were drowned together, with the two exceptions.

Local tradition around Cape Cod has another tale about the pirates, supported by the *Boston News-Letter* of April 29—May 16, 1717. In this version, the captive master of the Irish pinky ran her ashore while the pirates were all drunk below deck. The only trouble with this theory is that Captain Crumpstey of the pinky was taken aboard the *Whidah* at the time of capture, and so could not have been on the pinky when she was wrecked, ten miles away.

Returning to the story of the seven pirates from the pinky, Justice Doane no sooner had the pirates in the Barnstable jail than he heard of a second wreck, that of the *Whidah,* ten miles to the north of the pinky. It was Sunday before he arrived at the scene, where he found that Thomas Davis, the forced man, had visited the home of a Cape Codder named Harding, two miles away. The Cape Codder had shown the usual reaction to a shipwreck in those days, har-

nessing his horse at once and driving down with Davis to
the scene of the disaster.

With the Indian's help, the men made several trips from
the wreck to Harding's home, and it is believed Harding
had obtained the best merchandise from the cargo by the
time other Cape Codders arrived at the wreck. All day long
Saturday the mooncussers and beachcombers worked at their
interesting avocation, and when Sunday came, the beach had
been stripped clean of all important material from the cargo.
No gold or silver, as far as we can tell, had come ashore by
this time, as the bar was some distance off the shore. Dead
bodies, however, began to come up on the beach in alarming
numbers. Their disposal later caused Cyprian Southack
much trouble.

Reaching the beach Sunday morning, Justice Doane found
it picked clean, with the exception of a few articles seen
drifting ashore in the surf. Davis and Julian surrendered
to Justice Doane, and they joined the others at the Barnstable jail. Later in the week the nine men, under heavy
guard, were sent to Boston by horseback. The British sailors
from the wrecked frigate *Somerset* would have appreciated
this means of conveyance in 1778, when they were forced to
hike all the way from Cape Cod to Boston.

The next day the people of Boston were startled to hear
of the wreck of a pirate treasure ship on the sands of Cape
Cod, and Governor Samuel Shute went to bed that night
dreaming of pirate gold. He should have been warned by
the embarrassing experiences of his predecessor, Bellomont,
whose relationships with Captain Kidd caused him many
anxious moments. Shute's thoughts of great riches from the

buccaneer ship spurred him on, however. Issuing a proclamation to His Majesty's officers and subjects to take and hold all pirates, treasure and other goods from the wreck, Shute quickly looked over his available maritime gentry for a person of daring and courage who could go at once to the scene of the wreck.

Captain Cyprian Southack was the ideal mariner for this task. A very interesting sailor he was. Then in his fifty-sixth year, he was already planning the first real chart of Massachusetts Bay and its surrounding area, part of which is contained in this volume. He was artist, cartographer, fighter and seaman. Captain of the *Province Galley,* he made a sketch of Boston Light that is well known to antiquarians, while his chart of the coast was a necessity for all mariners for the next hundred years. Such were the accomplishments of this interesting Boston seaman of two centuries ago. We shall see, however, that they were of little avail against the traditions of the Cape Cod people, especially when it comes to a pirate shipwreck.

Captain Southack, now fully informed as to his mission, prepared to reach the scene. Hiring a small sloop, the *Nathaniel,* Southack left Boston on May 1, 1717. Five long and eventful days had passed since the wreckage was scattered by the storm along the great beach. Handicapped by a south wind, the sloop did not reach Cape Cod until the afternoon following its sailing, making six days in all since the wreck had occurred. Commandeering a whale boat at Cape Cod Harbor, he sent two men ahead to obtain horses in Truro. The men, mounted on horses, reached the scene of the wreck at seven in the evening, but it had been six long, profitable days for the men of Cape Cod, and by this time all movable goods from the *Whidah* had been stored in cellars, locked in barns and secreted in attics. Even Captain Williams of the pirate fleet had returned to join in the search for sunken booty, anchoring his ship off the shore and rowing in, but so many Cape Codders were there that he did not tarry long.

Meanwhile, Captain Southack started out in his whale boat from Provincetown Harbor, finally reaching Boat Meadow Creek in Orleans. From here he sailed up to a natural canal which at that time crossed Cape Cod. The canal was located between Orleans and Eastham, and has been called both Jeremy's Dream and Jeremiah Gutter. It is clearly indicated on Southack's map in this volume.

Captain Southack did not expect a cordial reception from the men of Cape Cod, and in this he was not disappointed. In his own words, he found the "Pepol very Stife and will not [surrender] one thing of what they Gott on the Rack." Caleb Hopkins of Freetown was very indignant, and the two men almost came to blows, while Samuel Harding, to whose house Thomas Davis had journeyed the morning of the wreck, said that Davis had ordered him not to part with any of the spoils from the sea. "I find the said Harding is as Gilty as the Pirates saved," were Captain Southack's conclusions.

The Governor allowed Southack extraordinary powers. He could "go into any house, shop, cellar, warehouse, room or other place and in case of resistance to break open any door, chests, trunks," or other objects to get the pirate goods. With all this authority, however, Cyprian Southack was un-

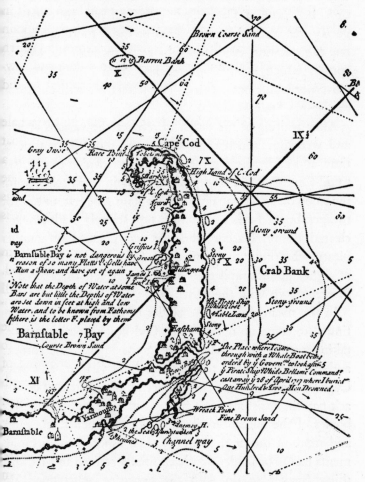

AUTHENTIC PIRATE TREASURE MAP, SHOWING LOCATION OF
BELLAMY'S TREASURE SHIP *WHIDAH*

able to gather much merchandise and in spite of all the time he spent at Cape Cod, comparatively little salvage goods ever reached Boston. That he did a thorough job no one can question, especially if he reads through the lengthy epistles which Southack dispatched from time to time to Governor Shute and others. The letters are still on file at the Boston State House.

After waiting at the beach to recover the various articles and wreckage which came up on the shore from time to time, and gathering together the material which one or two timid Cape Codders relinquished, Captain Southack sent for the sloop *Swan,* commanded by Captain Doggett, to sail the meager booty back to Boston. But scarcely had Doggett cleared Boston Harbor when he was pursued by another pirate, who promptly boarded the *Swan,* took goods valued at eighty pounds, and then allowed Doggett to proceed to Provincetown with the vessel.

In the meanwhile, as the bodies of the dead pirates continued to come up on the Cape Cod beach, some means of taking care of them had to be agreed upon. The coroner and his jury ordered the burial of the victims, and with Cyprian Southack right on the scene, he asked that Southack pay the expenses. The fighting and wrangling over the bodies of the buccaneers is almost beyond belief. As more and more of the dead pirates washed ashore, new arrangements had to be made. Southack finally refused to have anything further to do with the expenses, whereupon the coroner posted an attachment on some of the goods which Southack had just collected from the wreck, and received his money.

The attempts which Southack made to reach the treasure were exacting and tedious. Day after day he rowed out to the scene, trying to discern the bags of silver and gold down through the muddy waters, but since the heavy rain continued almost every day the water stayed muddy. He finally abandoned his search in the vicinity of the bar off the beach and returned to Boston with the goods he was able to secure. It is to be questioned whether Governor Samuel Shute profited much from this unusual adventure of the drowned pirates of Cape Cod. In his disappointment, he probably obtained little comfort from the fact that Governor Bellomont back in 1700 had concluded his experiences with Captain Kidd with even greater trouble and embarrassment.

The men accused of piracy, with the exception of Machconachy, who was evidently released at Cape Cod, were all taken to Boston and placed in jail there.

The pirates were allowed to languish in prison all that long summer of 1717. It was not until October 18 that they were brought to trial in the Admiralty Court at Boston. John Julian never came to trial, and was either let off or died in jail. Thomas Davis convinced the Court of his innocence of any wrong doing, and when pardoned sank to his knees on the courtroom floor, "thanked the Court and was dismissed with a suitable admonition." The others were found guilty.

Cotton Mather, who often visited the pirates in their jail cells, became so thoroughly convinced of the innocence of one of them, Thomas South of Boston, England, that he obtained a reprieve for him on November 2, thirteen days be-

fore the other six were executed. The unusual interest
Mather showed in the pirates is indicated in the good man's
diary for November 15, 1717, the day the last members of
the Bellamy crew were hanged:

15 G. D. There is good this day to be done, on a very solumn
Occasion. Six pirates were this day executed. I took a long and
sad walk with them, from the Prison, to the Place of Execution.
I successively bestowed the best Instructions I could, pray'd with
them, and with the vast Assembly of Spectators, as pertinently
and as profitably as I could.

The six pirates were Simon Van Vorst, of New York;
John Brown of Jamaica; Hendrick Quintor of Amsterdam;
Thomas Baker, also from Holland; Peter Hoof of Sweden,
and John Sheean of Nantes, France. On November 15, 1717,
they were taken down to the Charlestown Ferry, and there
rowed out to a scaffolding erected out over the water. Baker
and Hoof were penitent and humble. Hoof joined with
Van Vorst at the last minute in singing a Dutch psalm,
while John Brown broke out into furious oaths, but afterwards began to read from the prayer book. Then Brown
made a speech to the great assemblage.

"Beware of wicked living," said Brown to his listeners.
"Also, if you fall into the hands of pirates, as I did, have a
care into which country they come to." Then the scaffolding
fell, and the six outlaws of the sea met their fate.

After the execution Mather wrote a pamphlet on the in-
cident, but his regular printer refused to print it, so John
Allen printed 1200 copies of "A Brief Relation of RE-
MARKABLES in the Shipwreck of Above One Hundred

Pirates, Who were Cast away in the Ship *Whido,* on the Coast of New England, April 26, 1717." The book had a good sale, but is a very rare volume today.

His various sermons, pamphlets and discourses with the condemned men gave Mather a peculiar pedestal to occupy in the mind of the average pirate at sea. Cotton Mather later admitted that he learned of several victims of the men who had gone into piracy who were forced to curse Cotton Mather as part of their punishment. This strange ritual which befell those captured by pirates on the high seas must have disturbed Mather, for later in life when called by a pirate to pray for him, Mather said, "The Pyrates now strangely fallen into the Hands of Justice here, make me *the first man,* whose Visits and Counsils and Prayers they beg for." Nevertheless, his unusual interest in matters pertaining to pirates and their executions must have surprised some of the other good people of America's leading seaport.

As is usual in any discussion of fact which has been handed down from generation to generation, the *Whidah's* story is controversial in many parts. For example, no less a learned body than the Massachusetts Historical Society published in its 1793 *Collections* a story to the effect that the *Whidah* was actually decoyed, along with the rest of a pirate fleet, onto the shore of Cape Cod, because of the clever plans of the captain of a vessel who had been captured the day before.

The tale continues that a lantern was hung in the shrouds of one vessel, the snow, as the night was dark, and the entire fleet followed the snow * into the breakers and to disaster. Actually only two vessels were wrecked, the wine pinky and the *Whidah,* thus disproving the Historical Society *Collections* story.

The shifting sands often exposed the iron caboose of the *Whidah* on the outer bar at dead low tide. "Uncle Jack" Newcomb told Henry David Thoreau that he had seen the iron caboose at low tide many times but it is not believed that anyone has seen this section of the pirate chieftain's flagship above water since the 1860's. According to Perley, Thoreau and his companion found some of the treasure on the bar years ago.

Henry O. Daniels, a present resident of Eastham, Massachusetts, often walked the Cape Cod beach near the turn of the present century with Asa Cole, who found almost 300 coins of various denominations and sizes on the shore near the wreck of the *Whidah.*

John Howard Nickerson of Chatham found the ancient hull of the pirate ship *Whidah* in 1923, a short time after Seth Knowles had sold him a cigar box full of pieces of eight. Seth had dug up the coins in various places along the beach near the scene of the *Whidah's* wreck. Seth hadn't uncovered the money all at once, but had made it a practice to visit the beach after northeast storms. He'd come back to his home after every storm with a dozen or so pieces of eight. Finally he sold the entire collection, 578 coins, to John Howard Nickerson, who in turn disposed of them through his antique shop at Chatham. Those 578 coins rep-

---

* A snow is similar to a brig, but has a trysail mast close aloft the mainmast.

resent the greatest haul of silver pieces of eight in Cape Cod history.

Personally, I have spent the equivalent of a small treasure hoard at the scene of the pirate ship's wreck. There I erected a fifteen-foot diving platform as near as possible to that part of the *Whidah* which was said to contain the cannon. The weeks went by and the expenses mounted. Diver Jack Poole tried his best to salvage a substantial amount of gold or silver from the wreck, but a handful of pieces of eight worth at most one-fortieth of the cost of the operation was all he ever brought to the surface. We almost lost one boy by drowning when he attempted to swim ashore from the platform at high tide, and then a terrific storm hit which smashed the platform to pieces.

It is easy for a reader to wonder why the bulk of the treasure has not yet been found, but should he actually visit the scene and go out into the breakers where the operation has to be conducted, and be battered and smashed by the action of the sea, then his ideas might change. Indeed, it will be a very lucky treasure hunter who ever does more than pay expenses while attempting to find the elusive gold and silver still aboard the *Whidah*.

There are some doubters who do not believe that the *Whidah* ever was located. In their anxiety to detract from the importance of those who believe they discovered the *Whidah*, they feel that, starting with Cyprian Southack in 1717, everyone who claimed to have located the *Whidah* had found the wrong ship. It is their theory that the wreck now considered by many as the *Whidah* is another vessel entirely. Of course, their theory can never be proved, for even if they did find another ship, loaded with gold and silver, that would be no sign that that particular ship was the *Whidah*. At present there are four different groups at Cape Cod, each with its own idea of where the *Whidah* now lies.

John Light, of West Newton, Massachusetts, youthful diver of eighteen, became fascinated by the prospect of going down to visit the old wreck. After a careful study of the situation, he has given me a statement. As he is one of the few to visit the scene in full diving costume, his opinion should therefore be a relatively important one:

"I believe that the *Whidah* is a greater distance down the beach than the wreck which the average person believes is the old galleon, say 100 to 200 yards, and a little farther out away from shore. I also feel that the treasure from the *Whidah,* if it is there, can be salvaged. It is possible to use an air lift to create a suction which would bring up anything which is around the vessel."

Personally, it is my opinion that the sea will never allow any searcher to recover more than a small part of that great treasure which the *Whidah* carried when she went to her doom in the surf of Cape Cod. The great billows which constantly break at this part of the coast will cause all but the most determined treasure seekers to give up in despair after a few hours of being battered and tossed by the combers of Wellfleet. But the eager seekers will continue to come and match their wits against the sea, and all I can say is that I wish those who hope to find the pirate treasure the best of luck.

CHAPTER 4

Buccaneer Morgan's Treasure Cave

SIR HENRY MORGAN, called by many the greatest of all "the brethren of the coast," was a Welshman, born at Llanrhymmy in the year 1635. When a young man he journeyed to Barbadoes, where he fell in with a pirate named Mansvelt who was planning to equip a fleet and ravage the Spanish mainland. From that time on Morgan's name was associated by the Spaniards with everything in the way of murder, pillage, and piracy.

As the English government realized that Morgan was helping the British cause when he carried out his ruthless pillaging of the Spanish possessions, the English authorities didn't do too much to stop him. In 1665 he plundered the province of Campeachy, looted the island of Cuba, captured

New Providence Island, sacked Granada and burned Costa Rica.

In 1670 Morgan performed his most memorable feat, the sacking of Panama, entering the city from an angle which made the Spanish guns useless. After ravaging the city and obtaining rich spoils, he returned to his rendezvous at Chagres, where his men were awaiting the division of the booty. Then and there Morgan proved himself the double-dealer he really was, for he fled from Chagres with a handful of his most trusted associates, leaving the majority of his fellow buccaneers with only ten pounds apiece, deserted and forgotten, without ships or provisions.

Arriving in triumph at Port Royal, Jamaica, however, Morgan was given a vote of thanks by the Council of Jamaica for his successful expedition. Later several of his deserted followers reached Port Royal, where they openly accused Morgan of robbing them of their fair share of the booty. A new governor clapped Morgan into prison, and in April he was put in chains and sent back to England aboard the frigate *Welcome*. But the same false aura which surrounds many gangsters in America in modern times accompanied Morgan to England, where he was feted as a hero and the charges against him were quickly dismissed.

Henry Morgan was even powerful enough to sue William Crooke, who had published a book by Joseph Esquemeling which called Morgan what he really was, a buccaneer. The poor publisher had to pay two hundred pounds damage, and write a long and groveling apology.

Knighted as Sir Henry Morgan in November, 1674, he was sent back to the West Indies as Deputy Governor of Jamaica.

In 1681 Sir Thomas Lynch became Governor of Jamaica, and trouble began at once between Lynch and his deputy. One day Morgan damned the Jamaica Assembly in public, and was promptly suspended from office.

In April, 1688, he was reinstated by the King of England at the urgent request of the Duke of Albemarle, but he was already ill when he heard the good news. Sir Henry Morgan, buccaneer extraordinary, died of fever on August 25, 1688, and was buried with great honors at Port Royal.

Just before his fatal illness, Morgan had planned to journey across the Caribbean Sea to his former stamping grounds at Old Providence Island, where he had buried a very substantial part of his loot in a cave. His fever prevented him from carrying out his plans. If he ever told anyone else of this hoard in the cave, that secret-sharer never did recover it.

In 1710, twenty-two years after Henry Morgan had been buried with such pomp and ceremony at Port Royal, a baby boy was born at Bristol, England. Named Edward Seward, the child grew up to enjoy the life of a sailor. In the spring of 1733 Edward Seward went aboard his uncle's brig *Mary* as supercargo on a training cruise to Baltimore. After a long voyage in which he carried out his duties as supercargo and watched the cargo carefully, he returned to Bristol, where the young man found that he then had sufficient funds to get married. The girl of his choice was a Miss Eliza Goldsmith, also of Bristol. Edward Seward and Eliza Goldsmith were joined in matrimony on October 30, 1733.

When the brig *Mary* was again ready for trade, this time in the West Indies, Edward and Eliza went along for their honeymoon. Their first port of call was Jamaica, the very island on which Morgan had died forty-six years before. Then began a trading journey around the West Indies. The *Mary* cleared Pedro Bank and headed southwest, bound for Honduras. That very night a severe tropical hurricane lashed the entire area, and every time a sailor was sent aloft he was blown off into the sea to his death. Soon, bereft of all her sails, the brig drifted helplessly in the mighty gale. Several days went by without a letup in the storm's intensity. Then, in the early morning hours of December 30, the cry of "breakers ahead" was heard.

Soon the brig was caught in the trough of the sea, which pushed her toward the coral reefs ahead. The *Mary* struck, shivered, and came to a stop. The frightened captain lost his nerve completely, and ran around the deck shouting, "Look out for yourselves; look out for yourselves!"

The lifeboat was put over into the raging seas, and the captain and all his crew scrambled aboard, but after Seward and his wife had taken a glance at the angry waves they told the others to go off without them.

"You'll never live to reach shore," Seward shouted at the captain, but the others ignored him and pushed away from the brig. A moment later a great wave with a breaking crest rose out of the sea fifty yards beyond the terrified captain and his crew and gathered speed as it roared toward the beach. Smashing into the lifeboat, the giant wave swamped it, drowning every occupant. Edward Seward and his wife then realized that they were the only ones saved from this terrible disaster.

Almost at once the storm began to subside, the wind shift-

HENRY MORGAN

ing from northwest to southwest. Then a strange thing happened. The brig started to swing herself around toward the sea. Seward rushed for the tiller, reaching it just in time. As the brig slid clear of the reef, Edward steered her safely by another jagged ledge of coral bars, into an inlet half a mile away, and then beached her on a sandy shore in a lagoon. What had seemed a hopeless situation only two hours before had miraculously improved in this short space of time. The bride and groom found themselves alone on a deserted island.

From that moment on, the adventures of the young honeymooners resembled a combination of the Swiss Family Robinson story and what happened to Robinson Crusoe, with an amazing new climax thrown in besides. Everything seemed to combine to bring luck to the two adventurers and their dog, a King Charles spaniel which had stayed on the *Mary* with them.

After resting and getting food to eat, Seward began an exploration of the island, which he discovered was four miles long and slightly more than two and a half miles wide. After great effort in studying the various charts which he found in the ship's cabin, he rightly concluded that the island was none other than the location known as Old Providence, rendezvous of Henry Morgan himself. Even Morgan's Head was clearly indicated on the chart. The island where the *Mary* had been wrecked was actually the very island where Morgan had buried his treasure, but, of course, neither Edward nor Eliza could have known about this unusual fact.

After the shipwreck, Seward proved himself a master at planning. He soon had the surviving goats and fowls ashore. Then he planted several bags of seeds which were aboard. He was able to catch all the fish he needed, and the yams, melons, and pumpkins which grew wild gave him and his wife a balanced diet. He found several cases of wine on the brig, and whenever fresh meat was needed, the trusty little spaniel would kill a lizard, which was promptly cooked.

Month after month went by. One morning, more from boredom than anything else, Seward decided to explore the interior of a cave-like depression which he was using for storing goods. When he reached the back of the cave, he happened to notice certain indications that human hands had erected a barrier or wall there. He found a small fissure in the barrier. Evidently a storm, some years before, had broken through a man-made wall separating the front from the back of the cave, and tons of sand had been swept through a small opening which the sea had created. But in running out, the water evidently had exposed several canvas bags which held gold doubloons. When Seward caught a glimpse of the gold, he became tense with excitement. Smashing at the wall with a rock, he forced his way into the back of the cave, where he found himself in the presence of the old Morgan loot.

"Treasure!" he shouted to his wife, who was strolling with the spaniel a short distance away. "Come here, Eliza, in the back of the cave! I can't believe it!" Soon they were both eagerly opening the bags and boxes. Indeed, the treasure was greater than could be imagined.

As the couple dug into the booty, they were simply overwhelmed by what they found, and rightly so. There were thirty-six beautiful crucifixes stolen from Spanish cathedrals, twelve diamond-studded sword scabbards, forty golden chains, eight triangular altar pieces embossed with scriptural figures, and several cases of gold leaf.

There were also eighty crucifixes, fifty chains, twelve pairs of shoe buckles, and a variety of smaller items, all made of silver. Then there were two cases of rare perfumes. But the bulk of the treasure was twenty thousand golden doubloons, fresh from the mint, each then worth $18.

For the next few weeks Seward and his wife busily counted the money and sorted the rest of the treasure. But they realized that this wealth was of little value unless they could get off the island. The weeks went by, however, and no sign of rescue appeared.

The ship's telescope was still aboard the brig, and Seward often took it up to the top of Morgan's Head to watch for passing ships. Early one morning, he went to his observation post to watch the approach of a storm. Suddenly he noticed two tiny dots on the horizon.

"Eliza," he shouted. "Come quickly!" Soon they were both taking turns watching through the glass as the tiny specks became larger and larger. He eventually identified them as two canoes, with men in the canoes paddling like mad to escape the storm. On and on they came, and finally arrived at the beach. Seward took his blunderbuss and went down on the shore to greet them.

"Who are you," he asked.

"We—slaves—escape wreck two nights before. Help us, please."

And so it was that Seward accepted the company of six former slaves. He agreed to care for them, and they in turn would help carry out the affairs of the island. Seward and his wife, who had been living aboard the wrecked brig, now built a hut with the aid of the former slaves, and moved ashore with them. A fine island spirit developed, with Seward teaching the Negroes the English language.

With the help of the others, Seward erected a flagstaff high on Morgan's Head, so that a flag could be displayed should a British ship appear.

One day eleven months after their wreck, he noticed a Spanish brig chasing an English schooner toward the island. As both vessels passed close to the headland, Seward and his men fired upon the Spanish vessel, which fled at once. The English vessel sought the safety of the island.

Later, the Spanish brig returned and launched a small boat. Seward waited until the small boat was near shore, and then he and his men paddled out and captured the occupants. There was no opposition at all. After a reprimand, he let the Spaniards go.

The English schooner had been damaged by the fire of the Spaniards, and the vessel was run aground on the island and repaired. Seward and his wife decided that they would leave the island on the schooner, and had Morgan's treasure transported aboard. The former slaves were to run the island.

Sailing away from Providence Island, Seward and his wife reached Kingston, Jamaica, on March 12, 1735, eighteen months after they had left England. At Kingston he transferred 22,000 of the golden doubloons to a warship, which transported them back to England. He kept 8,000 of the doubloons, worth $144,000, with him, and sent $6,000 back to his six Negro friends on the island.

In England it appears that Seward's uncle, the owner of the wrecked brig, couldn't stand the good fortune which his nephew had encountered because of his shipwreck. The uncle ignored the fact that Seward had salvaged the brig and sent his representatives from Kingston over to Old Providence, where they repaired the ship and made it ready for sea. Then the uncle ordered stores put aboard to the cost of $2,000. He invited Seward to journey back home aboard the brig. Arriving in Bristol, Seward and his wife were greeted by all their friends. His uncle, however, billed him for $2,000 for the goods which Seward had not asked for, and also charged him and his wife $625 for the passage homeward.

But Seward didn't protest too much, for his account at the local bank then had a value of $600,000, all because of Henry Morgan's treasure of golden doubloons and the gold and silver dishes and ornaments.

In case any of you would like to visit Old Providence today, there probably are many other treasures on the island, but I doubt that you will be as lucky as Edward Seward was back in the year 1733, when he found a pirate treasure worth $700,000.

CHAPTER 5

Captain Harding's Fatal Voyage

ALL men who have followed the sea for any length of time have heard of the famous chart maker, Captain George W. Eldridge, who lived for over thirty-five years at Vineyard Haven, on Martha's Vineyard. The title was an honorary one.

Captain Eldridge spent many, many years sailing up and down the New England Coast, exploring various harbors and inlets and making his very useful surveys. During the course of his trips he uncovered countless true stories concerning activities of unusual interest along our Atlantic shores, but few tales can be said to equal the fascinating account of the brig *Splendid,* which Captain Eldridge often told to an intrigued audience at his home. When I first heard the story I visited Martha's Vineyard for the details, which I eventually obtained.

Late in the year 1846 the brig *Splendid* cleared from the port of Salem, Massachusetts. Her master, Captain Harding, was sailing around the Cape of Good Hope for the East Indies with an assorted cargo. Hidden away in a large, iron-bound oak chest in the captain's cabin were 60,000 silver dollars, in sixty large canvas bags, each bag containing one thousand dollars and weighing about fifty-six pounds.

The silver had been brought aboard because of a last-minute conference between the captain and the mate, Howard Walker. Captain Harding had locked the chest and hidden the key in a secret compartment in the cabin, but Walker soon found out where the key was.

The last-minute conference had been carefully schemed by the mate who intended to increase his wealth by dishonesty and murder. Walker, a former pirate, was about to enter the profession for a second time. He had brought aboard a private collection of drugs which he planned to use to his advantage on the first occasion that presented itself, and between the drugs and the silver dollars he contemplated a brilliant future for himself. If Captain Harding had ever even guessed what was in Walker's mind, he would have clapped the mate in irons and returned to port at once.

According to Captain Eldridge, the master of the *Splendid* was not too hard with his crew, but when Mr. Walker strode the quarter deck, it was a different story. His appearance was striking, for he was tall and thin, and had jet black hair. His long mustache and trim goatee were in marked contrast to the gray beaver hat which he always wore. His entire bearing was ominous and sinister, and the crew fell under his spell at once, paying far more respect to Walker than they did to easy-going Captain Harding.

Mr. Walker soon made it a point to have his meals with Captain Harding whenever he could, and by the time they were eight days at sea he had worked himself into Harding's good graces so that the mate began the habit of pouring the Captain's tea and coffee for him.

When they were ten days out he began to dope the beverages, and a week later was able to increase the drug until Captain Harding became so ill that he couldn't leave his bunk. The mate continued to give larger doses, until eventually the poor captain lived from day to day in a state of perpetual stupor.

Walker would visit Captain Harding regularly three times a day, pretending that he was reporting to his master on all details of the voyage, but actually the captain was too befuddled to comprehend anything. In actuality, the mate was in supreme command, and Captain Harding a doomed prisoner in the murderous control of his subordinate. For six and a half weeks this strange state of affairs continued, until the Cape of Good Hope was sighted and passed.

Meanwhile, members of the crew began to wonder what really was the trouble with Captain Harding. None of them was sick in any way, yet the captain evidently was seriously ill. Could he actually be as sick as was claimed?

One night a sailor slipped by the shuttered cabin window, and through a break in the shade could see the captain in his bunk, obviously dead to the world, while Mate Walker sat nearby on a stool, his head in his hands, gazing intently at the iron-bound strong box.

One morning, several days after the *Splendid* had left the Cape of Good Hope behind, Mr. Walker announced that Captain Harding was sinking rapidly. During all of the Captain's illness, the mate had not allowed anyone else to enter the cabin, and his rule was absolute and unquestioned.

The following night Mr. Walker increased the drug several times and served it to Captain Harding in a fresh brew of tea. Before midnight the captain was dead. Without question the mate had murdered his superior officer.

The next day, as is the custom when a vessel is far from land, Captain Harding's body was wrapped in a blanket, weighed down at the feet, and sewn into a tarpaulin. Then, with every member of the crew standing by, Mr. Walker began the funeral service at sea, a sad event indeed for all who have witnessed such an occasion.

But there were two significant factors in the next few hours, each noticed by the crew members.

First, when the crew had assembled on the quarter deck to pay their last respects to their former leader, Mr. Walker began reading a verse of scripture from the Bible. He finished and then signaled for the captain's remains to be slid off the plank which held them, over the rail and into the sea. As the canvas-wrapped body hit the water and disappeared, Walker's nerve broke for a brief moment, his entire frame was convulsed in a terrific shudder, and the Bible dropped out of his hands into the sea. Every member of the crew felt that this was indeed an ill omen, and returned to his post with a feeling of dread for the future.

The second strange factor was that, instead of moving his belongings to the captain's cabin, Mr. Walker, who was now Captain Walker in his own right, announced that he would remain in his old quarters. Incidentally, he never did sleep in the captain's bunk or use the former master's quarters. Because of this the crew members, a superstitious group, as most sailors are, began to wonder and talk among themselves.

On and on the *Splendid* sailed, until Port Moresby in the East Indies was reached. Then the anchors rattled down in the harbor, and the long voyage was ended.

Seventeen days later, with the entire cargo of the *Splendid* unloaded, Captain Walker began planning for the return voyage, scheming how he would get a substantial part of the $60,000 still aboard. He realized that some outsider would have to help him, and eagerly scanned the faces of newcomers who entered the local waterfront tavern. One morning he decided that he had found the man he was after.

The man in question was Captain A. P. Johnson, master of the full-rigged ship *Dorothy Alice,* who was on the eve of sailing to the United States. Johnson was a small, wiry, weather-beaten individual, and Walker felt that here indeed was a man he could trust.

Captain Walker drew Johnson aside, and told him that he had discovered a pirate treasure worth $60,000. He explained that he would be under suspicion should he return to the States with it, but that if another American sea captain could land it somewhere in the States, he would split the dollars half and half. Suspicious at first, Johnson saw the plan in a much rosier hue after a few hours of indulgence and affability, and before the two captains parted, all arrangements had been settled. However, the captain of the *Dorothy Alice* gave Walker a final word of warning.

"Captain Walker, I've listened to your story and promise that I'll carry out my part of the agreement. But if I ever discover that you have deceived me, or if you ever reveal my part of the affair to anyone, I'll come after you and get you if it's the last thing I ever do. Mark me well!"

Somewhat taken back by the intensity of Johnson's statement, Walker attempted to assure the other that no deceit or trickery had been or would be practiced. But the crafty captain had been duly impressed by Johnson's warning.

On the next misty evening Walker sent all his crew ashore except the watchman of the *Splendid,* into whose grog Walker had dropped a small amount of dope, so that the custodian of the ship was soon sleeping soundly.

Ten minues later a jolly boat from the *Mary Alice* came alongside the *Splendid,* and the sixty money bags were transferred within two hours. An equal weight of rocks was placed in the captain's oak chest. At dawn the *Mary Alice* was made ready for sea, sailing with the tide that morning. As far as Johnson could tell, no one still in port knew of the transfer of the money.

For the next few weeks Walker made it a point to haggle and bargain conspicuously for the cargo of pepper and spices which was slowly being put aboard. Meanwhile, various other ships from all ports of the world entered and left the harbor, and the *Mary Alice* was soon forgotten. So, when Captain Walker completed the loading of his ship, and took the native dealers aboard to make his payments, no one even remembered that Walker and Johnson had exchanged words one morning in the local tavern.

Setting the stage as only he could do, Walker had the merchants sitting around the cabin when he ordered his crew to open the iron-bound strong box before them. The key was produced, the padlock thrown open, and the lid swung back.

"Empty!" shouted Captain Walker. "We've been robbed!"

There was terrific confusion for the next few hours, while the island was alerted and possible thieves were hunted down. But of course, nothing of the treasure was ever found in the East Indies, for by this time the 60,000 silver dollars were sailing merrily somewhere off the Cape of Good Hope, bound back to Massachusetts, whence they had sailed a little over a year before.

The native merchants, anxious for the business, agreed to take Walker's signed notes instead of the cash which they sadly realized was not available, and Captain Walker, his ruse succeeding, sailed for home the following week. Reaching Salem several months later, he warped his vessel in at Derby Wharf, reported the strange occurrences aboard the *Splendid* to the local police and the ship's owners, and was paid off.

Arriving in Boston, he went to the ship chandlery to meet, by previous agreement, with Captain Johnson. Here he found instead a letter awaiting him from the master of the *Mary Alice*. The letter explained that Johnson had anchored in the harbor of Vineyard Haven several months before, gone ashore with $30,000 and buried it in an obscure section near the beach at East Chop Light. Captain Johnson had enclosed a well-drawn map. He ended his letter with a final warning to Walker not to reveal their secret.

Pirate Walker journeyed at once down to the island of Martha's Vineyard, found East Chop Light, made friends with the Keeper and his family, and was seen hiking up and down the nearby shore. Then, as quickly as he had come, he left the island. He had found and inspected his treasure, but realized that he would have to wait until more time passed before beginning his digging.

Eighteen months later, Pirate Walker returned to Martha's Vineyard and established quarters at the home of one Dennis Dexter, a fisherman. He then visited Nicholas Brown, who lived nearby, and explained his mission. He wished to move his treasure away from Martha's Vineyard to the mainland, where he planned to settle near Falmouth, Cape Cod. Brown agreed to help and to secure several men who would join with them in transferring the silver. Each man, Walker promised, would receive $500 for one night's work.

Two nights later the group rowed out to a point opposite the treasure, went ashore and dug up the hoard. After several trips they had transferred all of it to Captain Brown's *No Man's Land* vessel, a strange craft rigged with two masts and no bowsprit, vaguely similar to the Johnny Wood boats of the Maritime Provinces.

A course was set for Falmouth on the mainland. By two o'clock the hustling men had anchored the vessel, sent ashore the treasure and dug out a shallow pit near the sandy beach. Before the sun arose all the money had been buried, and Captain Walker hastily placed a red scarf around the base of the nearest tree, planning to return later and familiarize himself with the spot, for it was his purpose to buy that particular part of the beach and build a home near the treasure, so that he could conveniently draw on the money each week.

Captain Walker paid off his fellow conspirators, giving them each a half-peck measure of silver dollars, and they sailed back to Martha's Vineyard and scattered to their various homes, sworn to secrecy.

Back in Falmouth, pirate Walker decided to visit the local village and inquire about the property he wanted to own, but was maddened to learn that the local inhabitants had found out all about the treasure. One of their number, returning from a fishing trip, had pulled his dory up on the nearby beach and started across the fields for his home. Noticing a brilliant red scarf tied to a tree, he became curious and searched around the area. He soon spotted the freshly spaded earth nearby. On investigating further, he uncovered the money bags.

Rushing into town, he told the authorities, who commandeered a wagon and team, returned to the spot, and loaded the treasure aboard. Two hours later it was safely locked up in the local bank, and all crossroads in the vicinity were posted with signs asking for the owners of the treasure to step forward and claim it.

The ship owners of Salem soon learned of the affair and sent a representative down to the scene, where it was soon discovered that the money bags were indeed their own. The natives told the Salem men that pirate Walker had been in the vicinity. Although he tried to return to Martha's Vineyard to wait before claiming the treasure, he was apprehended in Vineyard Haven, taken back to Falmouth, and made to confront his former employers. Seeing that the game was up, he confessed what he had done, implicating the men who had helped him move the treasure, and each was forced to give up his share of the spoils. However, when the owners asked Captain Walker where the rest of the money was, his knowledge that Captain Johnson would return and seek him out, whatever might happen, sealed his lips, and he refused to identify his unknowing accomplice.

Walker was sentenced to Charlestown's State prison for twenty years for robbery and piracy on the high seas. Nothing was ever said or done about the obvious murder of Captain Harding, although the authorities felt that Pirate Walker was to blame for that as well.

Pirate Walker died in State's prison during the War between the States, a man who almost succeeded in as daring and dastardly a scheme as has ever been attempted against Massachusetts men and ships.

CHAPTER 6

Adventures in Bermuda

I HAD flown from Sable Island to Florida, from fabulous Oak Island in Nova Scotia to Ocracoke Island. But I had yet to explore the mysteries of Bermuda, that lonely collection of islands more than 650 miles out to sea. Eventually my wife and I made arrangements to fly there in a Pan American four-engined Constellation named the *Donald McKay,* and in it we left the United States one bright March morning in 1948, with Captain James O'Neal at the controls.

As our plane climbed higher and higher, I considered my three important objectives in Bermuda. The first two involved the investigation of buried treasure and the third involved research into the career of Captain John Lusher.

I wouldn't complain, of course, if I happened to come acros
one or two other interesting stories.

Seated next to me was Anna-Myrle, my wife, intensel
excited by the actuality of flight—and well she might hav
been. On all sides of us there were cloud banks of al
shapes and sizes, forming mountains and canyons and
islands is the sky. It seemed that we were playing a gi
gantic game of tag with these beautiful, fleecy formations
Suddenly we came out into an area fairly free of clouds
There was a sunny blue sky overhead, but far below us
about a mile above the sea, were small clusters of individua
clouds, and each contour was faithfully reproduced in
shadow on the blue-green water below.

We landed at Kindley Field, Bermuda, at four o'clock
that afternoon, Bermuda time. It was cooler than we had
hoped, but an hour later we were comfortable and warm

The following morning, I visited the library in Hamilton
and delved into Bermuda's history for several hours. The
treasure clues which I obtained there were numerous and
exciting. I learned, for example, that in 1726 a great treasure was dug up at Cooper's Island, consisting of twenty
gold tankards, twenty-five silver tankards, one hundred and
eighteen gold and silver receiving dishes, over two hundred
gold plates, thirty-five hundred doubloons and two thousand Joes. A doubloon is a gold coin worth now from sixty
to one hundred dollars and a Joe is a Portuguese coin now
valued at twenty dollars.

But it is at Saint George's Island that much of the ro-
mance and mystery of Bermuda still lingers. In the year
1815, when young John Davenport of England arrived at

Bermuda, he founded a business at Saint George's, selling dry goods and sundry items. Soon Davenport was negotiating with the British garrison for the contract to sell beef, and before ten years had elapsed, he was supplying the army with everything Bermuda could furnish. He then noticed that many a sea captain who entered Saint George's harbor was financially embarrassed for lack of cargo. Davenport advanced several of these captains money with which to sail home, taking a mortgage on part of their ships as security.

It was not long before Davenport became the most influential man on the island. He secretly amassed a substantial fortune from his various enterprises. Trusting neither Bermuda nor English banks, he devised an unusual method of concealing his wealth. He obtained a trustworthy carpenter and had him build fifty arrowroot kegs. Davenport took one of the kegs and placed it in his room. When he had it filled with gold and silver, he carried it down into his cellar to be stored. Then he replaced the full keg with an empty one in his room and repeated the process of saving. This happened several times each year. Davenport kept the only key to the cellar in a secret hiding place.

As he grew older, Davenport became more and more obsessed with the possibility of robbery. Finally he decided to remain at home continuously to guard his treasures. During the last year of his life, he and his trusted servant Joseph spent most of their time in the cellar, boring a hole in each keg in turn to make sure its contents were still gold and silver.

Finally Davenport died and the servant revealed his

secret to the old man's sons. Arrangements were made with
the government to examine and take over the treasure hoard
in return for bills on the London exchange. And what a
strange ritual this arrangement necessitated! Every morning Robert Davenport, the eldest son, ordered a new keg
brought up from the cellar, taken into the dining room, and
emptied on the great table. After the checking had been
completed, another keg was brought up, and then another,
until finally, fifty-eight days after the counting began, the
last keg was taken from the cellar.

Saint George's was a small town, and money bought
much more in the days before 1850 than it does now. It
was a fabulous marvel to the natives that no less than $400,-
000 in gold and silver was taken upstairs from Davenport's
cellar. This, by the way, was one of the largest miser's
hoards ever discovered anywhere.

One of the highlights of our trip to Bermuda was a de-
lightful visit with a woman of sixty-four years who had in
her younger days discovered a hidden treasure. Anna-
Myrle and I were strangers to her, and when I mentioned
mutual friends, we needed no further introduction.

"Well, young man," this woman began, "just what is it
you'd like to know about me? You want me to tell you
how I found gold, isn't that it?" When I nodded in agreement, she smiled and continued:

"I'd better begin at the beginning. Back when I was
eight or nine years old, in the 1890's, I was a husky young
lassie. My father ran a small boarding house over on
Trunk Island, in Harrington Sound. At that time the Mus-

sons owned the island. Perhaps they were pirates way back. Father was a retired sea captain and never had more than eight or nine guests. In those days, although I was very young, I could do the work of three women, and father knew it.

"I remember the first day that Mr. Doughty came to the boarding house. All that I recall about him now is that he came from the States and that his costume was most unusual. The nearest approach to it I've seen is the famous one-piece siren suit which Winston Churchill wore during World War II.

"Well, Mr. Doughty was always interested in getting sea shells. He seemed fascinated by them, so one night I said to him, 'If you want some flat plate shells, I'll take you over to Hall's Island early tomorrow morning.' Mr. Doughty quickly agreed, and at four the next morning we met at the beach. I slid the boat into the water, and Mr. Doughty sat down in the stern. He was pretty helpless, or he pretended to be, so I did the rowing.

"We landed at Hall's Island, about three-quarters of a mile across the Sound, and pulled the skiff up on the shore. Reaching the crevice which led down to the hidden cave where the flat plate shells were, I warned him against climbing down into the opening. He was a big man, Mr. Snow, weighing about as much as you do, over two hundred pounds.

"I went down alone and a moment later landed on the edge of the little beach, where I soon found several shells. When my eyes became accustomed to the dark, I noticed a large box or chest jammed into the rocky crevice far back in the cavern. It was an iron sea chest about three feet long, eighteen inches high, and two feet deep. I tried to open it, but the lid would not yield.

"I shouted back up to Mr. Doughty, 'Some fool person has dropped a trunk down here, and I can't move it or open it up to save me.'

"He peered down through the crevice and called, 'We can go back and get a chisel.' But I knew I had to get breakfast and wash the breakfast dishes. We returned to Father's house, and planned to row back that afternoon.

"It was almost four o'clock before we reached the island again, and I had to work fast. With the chisel I finally sheared off the hinges on the back of the chest, but try as I might, the lock could not be forced. So I pried and pried, and eventually the back of the chest cover pushed up from the chest itself.

"The first thing which caught my eye was a peculiar dagger, not straight-edged, but curved in and out. It was very rusty, and the handle was actually longer than the blade. Beautiful stones were on the handle—blue, green and red. I know now that they were rubies and emeralds.

" 'Someone must have had someone's head cut off!' I shouted up through the crevice to Mr. Doughty, who was peering anxiously down at me. By this time the tide had come in a little, and I was standing in water three or four inches deep. I only had one dress and one pair of shoes in those days, and it was quite serious if I ruined my shoes.

"Underneath the dagger I found what appeared to be a Mason's apron, made from the skin of a goat. Then I noticed that all along the top of the chest, on shelves, were small boxes. I opened one and found it contained coins. I didn't know enough about money then to tell whether the coins were gold or silver, but I pulled off my apron, which I still wore, and piled up the pieces in the apron. Soon they made quite a number, and when I tried to lift them the apron wouldn't budge.

"'Send down your fish line,' I called to Mr. Doughty, and ten minutes later he had hoisted the heavy money up out of the cavern at Hall's Island. After replacing the iron cover to the chest, I climbed out as fast as I could. I'd be late getting supper, and Father would make trouble. Father was all right unless we upset his schedule, and I knew pretty well how much he would stand. Mr. Doughty was to keep the money and the dagger in his room, and we were to tell Father after we got the rest of the treasure.

"We landed back at the boarding house just in time for supper, and that night I went to bed early—I had done a lot in one day. The next day it rained pitchforks, and since, as I told you, I only had one set of clothes and had to keep it for best, I couldn't go out at all. Father rowed Mr. Doughty over to the mainland during the day and when he returned that evening without Mr. Doughty, I mustered up my courage to ask a question.

"'Father, where's Mr. Doughty?'

"'Oh, he's gone away for a few days. He didn't say whether or not he would come back, but I don't think he will.' And that is the way I lost my fortune. The next few days were rainy, but when I finally had a chance, I rowed over to Hall's Island and went down into the crevice. Nothing remained; everything had been taken.

"I never could understand how Mr. Doughty managed to get the rest of that treasure. He couldn't row a boat, he didn't know how to swim, and yet he went away and the treasure went with him. How did he do it? I have puzzled about that for over fifty years, and I haven't worked out a solution yet. What do you think happened, Mr. Snow?" She paused, sat back in her chair, and waited for my answer.

I gave the matter considerable thought, and then decided that I had worked out a possible solution.

"Perhaps Doughty hired a boatman to take him over to the island and arranged for him to come back two hours later. He brought along two empty suitcases, and he stripped down to a bathing suit and thus was able to squeeze through the crevice. The fact that the money and the chest disappeared proves that he did get through. Next he filled the suitcases with the rest of the money, brought them down to the shore, and pulled out the iron chest. He tied up each article and then climbed to the top of the crevice and pulled it out." As I talked I warmed up to the theory myself.

"Then the boatman returned, and two suitcases and the empty chest were put aboard. Halfway between Hall's Island and what is now the shore, near the Harrington House, the iron chest was dropped down into the water, where it may still be today. Doughty left Bermuda by the next ship and lived happily ever afterwards on his ill-gotten gain.—Well, how do you like that solution?"

"No, Mr. Snow, that couldn't be what happened because there was no one he could hire to row him. I'll probably never know what happened to the bulk of the treasure I found, but I did save a few pieces of gold and silver. And

I want to give a piece of silver to your wife and a piece of gold to you." And this kind, entertaining lady of Bermuda was true to her word.

"Now I don't mind if you tell the story," she said as we left, "but keep my name out of it. I want you to promise me that." I gave her my faithful promise that we would never reveal her name.

"What if someone wants to write you suggesting a solution to the mystery? What if Mr. Doughty is still alive? Would you like to hear about it?"

"Of course I would, but let them write to you, Mr. Snow. You just send the letter along to me here in Paget, and I'll answer it if it rings true."

And that is what we agreed to do. That afternoon we went down to the Harrington House and looked across at Hall's Island. It was pouring rain, and those who saw us staring out into the sound at the deserted hummock of an island probably wondered at our interest. We saw the dim outline of a crevice and wondered if it was the one which had held the treasure chest. On my next trip to Bermuda I'll try to settle that mystery.

This treasure story concerns a young Negro, Russell Levi Pearman, of Victoria Street, Hamilton. I telephoned him one day during a driving rain, and he volunteered to meet me in town where I was doing some research at the time.

"I understand that you discovered a substantial amount of gold in a very peculiar fashion," I began.

His answer was direct and to the point.

"Would you like to hear the whole story?"

I answered that I certainly would, and he began to speak, his calm voice and his ready vocabulary lending added charm to the narration.

"I am a furniture or desk maker by trade, and on February 22, 1938, I was dismantling a desk which I had bought from my uncle, George Richardson, who lived for many years on Saint David's Island. I was planning to use parts of the desk to repair another which I believed to be of greater value. My uncle's desk was thirty-six inches wide, forty-two inches high, and about twenty inches deep. It was made of walnut and soft pine, but termites had consumed most of the soft pine.

"As I removed a section of the desk, I noticed a thin piece of wood in the center pigeon hole. When I removed it, I found a cavity or pocket in back.

"Of course, this surprised me, and I reached in carefully to discover if anything might be there. My hand touched paper first, and then I made my discovery—a hoard of gold coins, each piece wrapped in paper, the paper marked with the weight of the coin and the value.

"After sorting the coins, I found that they were of fifty-seven varieties, dating from the early 1700's to 1820. The 1820 piece was a Brazilian doubloon. Most of the other coins were either Portuguese or Spanish, with a few German and several Italian pieces. Many of the coins were counterstamped to denote the West Indian island where they had been in circulation. Without question, the careful way they were wrapped indicated that they were a collector's hoard."

It was indeed a colorful story which this modest Hamilton

Negro told me, and I asked him if he had ever learned who had secreted the hoard in the old desk.

"I have never found out whose treasure it was," he replied. "Not only that, I have never found out in what country several of the coins were minted. Even the experts were unable to identify them. When I went to New York City and showed them to several numismatists, they put the coins on exhibition at the Chase National Bank."

"Well, what did the Government take from you for the treasure trove?" I asked Russell Pearman, and he smiled in return.

"That's the best part of it all. Since the money was in a desk, it was not legally treasure trove. Treasure has to be under ground, and therefore I didn't have to pay the Government anything. The treasure was worth slightly more than $10,000. When I reported it to the Bank of Bermuda, it created quite a sensation. Everyone on the island started pulling apart his old desk, but mine was the only one which held golden coins."

"Would you like to sell me one of the coins?" I asked hopefully. "You see, I, too, have found buried treasure, and would like to add one of your coins to my collection."

"I'm sorry," he answered, "but we only have a third of the 151 coins left. My wife says that we have enough money, so I am not going to sell any more of the gold." And Mr. Pearman stuck to his statement. We shook hands in farewell, and I had finished my interview with a very lucky young man of Bermuda.

Back in Boston my friend Dick Johnson had told me

about some coins picked up on the Bermuda shore when he had been visiting there the previous year. Dick remembered a brief reference in the local paper at the time. Naturally, I wanted to meet the person who had found the coins, and I tried all the usual channels of information. Although we had asked almost everyone we had met and had been given several leads, for various reasons the leads proved unfruitful.

One day we were trying to locate a Mr. Perenchief, who had photographed Captain John Lusher, the diver. I wished to have a picture of the old diver and I had been told I could find Mr. Perenchief at the Bermuda News Bureau. Arriving there, I was received by the office boy who told me that Mr. Perenchief was busy at the tennis matches and would not be available.

The next day I returned and was told Mr. Perenchief would be back shortly, so I chatted with the office boy again. His name, it seemed, was Robert Repose. When I showed him the piece of eight which I always carry in my pocket, he said that he, too, had a piece of eight which he had found on the bathing beach the year before.

"Why, you're the boy I've been looking for all week!" I exclaimed. "I want you to tell me about it."

"Well, it wasn't much. Father and I went in swimming one day down at the beach and Father picked up an old metal disc and was about to chuck it away. He had found it in the rocks and sand, among what seemed to be the remains of a chest. Then I picked up another round metal piece, and we decided to scrape off the stuff on it and find out what the piece was. We took both discs of metal home and found they were silver coins. One was dated 1742 and the other 1745—both were pieces of eight."

"I'd like to take your picture with the coin," I told Robert. "Would you be able to go home and get it?" Robert readily agreed, and half an hour later I photographed him holding up his precious treasure coin.

"Everything happens to me since I started working for the News Bureau!" he exclaimed. "Will you really have my name in your new book?" I told him that I would not leave it out. As I drove away, the last I saw of Robert Repose was his excited face with a wide grin on it. Without question Robert and his father, August Repose, had come across the remains of a treasure chest. Probably the rest of the silver is within a few yards of the place where they found those two pieces of eight on the Bermuda beach.

The principal reason that Bermuda had beckoned, I must truthfully admit, was the unusual number of treasures reported on its various islands. Ireland Island, Cooper's Island, Hall's Island and Saint George's Island—all are locations of secret buried treasure.

When my wife and I had enjoyed sightseeing, hiking and swimming, and our aerial survey of the islands was complete, we were in the proper mood for that subject which has fascinated so many: buried treasure. I wish I could reveal the details of each experience we had. However, I have given my word not to violate certain confidences for reasons which I believe will become apparent.

We had metal detecting equipment of a highly sensitive nature with us. The detector reacts, of course, to metals other than gold and silver with considerably greater frequency. On the beach it often located iron spikes in fragments of old wreck timbers buried a few feet below the surface. This didn't disappoint us; no one should look for buried treasure and expect to find it. I have never expected to find any, and when I did, it came as a pleasant, overwhelming surprise.

At Bermuda the metal detector has been used on many occasions but without success as yet. I firmly believe that the day will come when detectors will locate both sunken and buried treasure. Twelve million dollars still remain within twenty miles of Hamilton itself—and that is no crack-brained estimate but the cold deductions of one who has made a lifelong study of the situation.

Since the sixteenth century the mighty Spanish plate fleets had used the islands of Bermuda as an important sea mark on their journeys to Europe from South America. In some years they carried as much as $21,000,000. Hurricanes frequently sent one of the treasure galleons to the bottom, and the locations of many of these wrecks were known in general.

Moreover, the earlier English settlers at Bermuda found many evidences of the wreckage of several Spanish galleons. By the law of averages, the hulls of some must be located not too far from the islands themselves.

On the night of September 13, 1621, the *San Antonio*, a Spanish galleon, hit a coral reef barely nine miles to the west of Bermuda. The seventy members of the ship's company finally reached Mangrove Bay, Bermuda, where they were discovered by the alarmed inhabitants. Suspecting an invasion, the Bermudians notified Governor Nathaniel Butler. When Butler investigated, he learned that the Spaniards were castaways and gave them food and shelter. He claimed later that he acquired from the Spanish captain a deed allowing him to salvage the *Antonio* for his own enrichment because of the generous treatment he had given the shipwrecked men.

But when the Spaniards from the *Antonio* finally reached London, they complained at once to their representative, Count Gondomar. The survivors told the Count that they not only had been treated shabbily in Bermuda but actually had been robbed by the Bermudians of valuables saved from the disaster. Count Gondomar made the most of the situation by writing an official communication to the Bermuda colony, listing the complaints one by one. The affair was finally brought to the attention of the Star Chamber, but no action was ever taken on the alleged ill-treatment of the shipwrecked Spaniards.

Governor Butler went to work salvaging the treasure from the *San Antonio*. He knew that it was there—the Spaniards had given him full details of the gold, silver and merchandise aboard. Week after week his men tried to bring the treasure to the surface, but as far as we know it is still there today. The Governor never recovered more than a few cannon from the wreck.

In the book which he wrote a short time later, *History of the Bermudaes,* Governor Butler mentions several other Spanish ships which were wrecked in the vicinity of the islands. Whether the great Henry Morgan, despoiler of Panama, also visited Bermuda to bury treasure is a debatable point. Many think so. Those who maintain this theory are equally certain that Morgan never returned to get that substantial treasure. Perhaps some enthusiast with a metal detector may yet find Morgan's millions on Bermuda's sandy shores. But anyone who expects to take gold off the islands without paying a treasure-trove tax will be doomed to disappointment. And the tax is a very substantial one on the Islands of Bermuda!

The day I visited William Zuill, author of *Bermuda Journey,* I asked him if he had ever heard of Captain John Lusher.

"Why, yes," Will Zuill answered, adjusting his glasses so that he could check some notes. "You must go out and see John Lusher. He was formerly a diver, and was interested particularly in the ancient Spanish treasure galleons. He's pretty old now, and I think that he is living at the Packwood House, in Somerset. By all means go over and visit him."

That, indeed, was a good clue, and we lost no time in driving over to Somerset. There we found that John Lusher had been transferred to the poorhouse two years previously.

Finally we were knocking at the door of the poorhouse. "I would like to speak with Mr. Lusher, if it is possible," I began to the woman who answered our summons.

"Goodness gracious, man, what do you mean? Poor old Mr. Lusher's been dead eighteen months or so!" This rather took the wind out of my sails, and I fell back a few paces and muttered my apologies. I am afraid the woman who runs the poorhouse thought I was having fun with her by asking to speak to a dead man.

As we went back down the lane and passed the old Saint James graveyard, three Negroes were walking toward us. Acting on a hunch, I decided to question them.

"Good-morning, gentlemen," I began. "I wonder if you could give me a little information." I then told them that my purpose was to find out what I could about the career of Mr. John Lusher, who had died in the poorhouse some time during the fall of 1946.

"Yessuh, mam, we can tell about Mr. Lusher," began the youngest of the three men. "He was a good man, about eighty-five years old when he died, and we all liked him. Yes, we certainly did. Why one day—"

"May I be privileged to say a few words?" broke in another Negro, who spoke in a much lower tone of voice. "Mr. Lusher did reside at the Packwood House earlier, but in his later years he lived up here. He was a wonderful man."

He went on to tell me what he knew about Lusher, and before our conversation was over I had several important clues which led from Somerset to Saint George's Island and back again to Hamilton. A conversation with Mr. Leon Fox in Saint George's and a story by Carol Booker in the *Bermudian* for August, 1946, finally completed my material on this colorful deep-sea diver, Mr. John Lusher of Philadelphia and Bermuda.

John Lusher was born at Bermuda in 1854. He always was a diver, although during certain periods of his life he was active in other work. In his youth he moved to Philadelphia, but in 1912 the cold winters finally sent him back to the birthplace he loved, Bermuda. On his return he began the building of a forty-foot boat which may still be seen at Saint George's. The boat was called the *Endeavor* and its name is appropriate—it took thirty-two years to build.

But Lusher's diving experiences interested me more than any other of his many achievements. One of his diving exploits was an expedition out to an ancient galleon, many miles from Bermuda. Arriving at the location, he went down in his diver's equipment and found the wreck without too much effort. There he discovered that coral encrustations had grown to rocklike consistency over the treasure room, and he sailed to the nearest port to obtain blasting materials. On his return two weeks later, he found that his earlier visit must have been observed—a native gunboat was standing guard over the sunken ship. Captain Lusher learned later that others probably brought the treasure to the surface, but nothing to that effect was ever announced officially.

Another expedition of Captain Lusher's was at Cape Comet, over seven hundred miles from Bermuda in a southwesterly direction. He descended to the ocean floor to locate a wreck which had fallen apart from age. Prying off a fragment of the hull, he discovered loose gold, exactly as it had slid from a great chest many years before. Again a native gunboat appeared, and Captain Lusher was ordered to leave the vicinity almost at once. He did get some souvenirs of that particular dive, however. A short time afterwards he learned that the nearby island, a few hundred yards from the treasure ship, had been purchased by two thrifty Scotsmen who found the gold later.

A third expedition took place just a few miles off Bermuda itself. It was on this occasion that Captain Lusher was so seriously injured that he could never again dive in deep water. For years he had studied all the old charts and records he could find and had read carefully the accounts of several Spanish wrecks in Governor Butler's book. Finally he decided to try to locate the old *San Antonio,* wrecked in 1621. He equipped himself with the most modern devices he could obtain and started out in his little sloop accompanied by two helpers.

It took him many weeks before he found the hulk. Once located, he returned day after day to the ship. He discovered old cannon, fragments of silverware and pottery, and countless other articles, but no gold coins or pieces of eight. Finally one night he realized that his money was running low, so he determined to make one great effort the next day.

The morning dawned warm, clear and windless, and before ten o'clock he had gone overboard and was standing inside the cabin of the old ship. Hammering away slowly but surely, for any movement under water is by necessity a labored one, John Lusher suddenly crashed through what appeared to be a bulkhead and another room was revealed.

"Can this be the stronghold of the ship?" Lusher wondered, and hacked away at the hole to enlarge it to the size of his body. At last he was able to lower himself down into the opening, where he could feel the shapes of what seemed to be treasure chests. Smashing his giant sledge against one of the trunks, he crushed in the cover, and quickly knocked it aside. He was right. The entire top of the chest was filled with what appeared to be either doubloons or pieces of eight.

In his eagerness to inspect the coins, he completely forgot the dangers which constantly threaten all deep-sea divers. He grabbed two of the coins and tried to scrape them against each other, but in so doing he had to release his hold on the life line. Just then his foot slipped in the sludge and evidently entered a small cavity in the treasure room. A second later a great weight crushed his instep and he thought that one of the chests had fallen on his foot. Reaching down, he was horror-stricken to find that he was in the grasp of a giant sea clam, two feet across and weighing hundreds of pounds. He was trapped far under water by this relentless creature which had never been known to release a victim.

Agonizing, excruciating pains were running through his leg as the giant clam slowly began to crush the bones of his foot. Then an idea came to him. He forced his heavy iron hammer into the remaining crevice of the clam's shell until the creature, with a tightening grip, caught the hammer and held it firmly. But the clam had already reduced Captain Lusher's foot to a hideous pulp. It is probable that he fainted at this point. He remembered awakening what seemed to be a short time later with a numbing sensation running through the whole of his leg.

Realizing that he would have to act immediately or die within a few moments, Lusher braced himself with his other foot and gave a violent tug on the life line as a signal to be hauled up. Steadying himself for the coming ordeal, he watched the line tighten. Soon the line jerked at his body, and its tugging threatened to cut him in two. At last he was ready for the supreme effort. With great pain, he pushed away from the galleon's timbers with all the strength left in his good leg and slowly but surely squeezed what remained of his other foot through the small opening. At this moment Lusher fainted for the second time. Half an hour later he regained consciousness on the deck of his vessel.

"What do you want us to do?" his frightened helpers asked him.

"Weigh anchor, hoist the mainsail, and start for a doctor on St. George's at once."

Lusher collapsed again and four hours later regained consciousness in a doctor's office. His leg had been treated and bandaged. The doctor told him that he would never again have the full use of his crushed foot. Lusher explained how he had barely avoided death.

"You're a lucky man to be alive then," the doctor told him. "You're the first person I've ever heard of who has escaped from the giant sea clam. How did you do it?"

Captain Lusher then told the astonished doctor of his strange experience in the cabin of the Spanish galleon. He did not reveal, however, that he had just come across the treasure.

"You can never dive again," the doctor warned, but in this he was mistaken.

Captain John Lusher, broken and crippled by his experience, did shallow water diving until he was seventy years of age. But never again did he venture out to the scene of his dangerous escape from that terror of the ocean bottom, the giant sea clam.

Those who knew him best said that he spent the rest of his life looking for a man who had three qualifications: first, youth and ambition; second, sufficient courage to dive far below the surface of the sea; third, honesty. Of course, Captain Lusher knew that a man with these three qualifications could be trusted with his great secret—the sunken treasure of a Spanish galleon.

John Lusher's crippled figure was a well-known sight in the streets of Bermuda for many years. His long white hair and bushy beard almost encompassed his ruddy face but did not detract from his alert blue eyes. Often toward the end of his life, he stopped to rest on one of the tombs of the Saint James churchyard, where, surrounded by the boys and girls of the neighborhood, whom he had grown to love, he would dream again as he told of his adventures under the surface of the sea.

But he never found the man for whom he was searching. John Lusher, his mission unaccomplished, died at the little Somerset poorhouse, overlooking Margaret Bay. Perhaps some day a youthful reader will follow in the footsteps of this ancient Bermudian patriarch and tempt the fortune which led Captain John Lusher to the very gates of wealth and then allowed him to die in poverty.

CHAPTER 7

Pirate Blackbeard's Treasure

Without question Edward Teach, alias Blackbeard, was the most notorious, despicable and ruthless pirate who ever slit a throat or carried off a woman prisoner. His treasures are reported up and down the Atlantic Coast, and in at least one instance they have been found. But it is also almost certain that the great bulk of Blackbeard's riches is buried in the sands of some lonely island, far from the reach of the average searcher.

During World War II, when I had been sent away from the North African campaign to a convalescent hospital in Bristol, England, I was interested to discover that this pleasant British seaport was the birthplace of Edward Teach.

103

Blackbeard, the greatest cutthroat of them all, was born at Bristol, in the year 1690.

By the time he had reached his teens, Blackbeard was already sailing the high seas under the command of a cold-hearted villain named Benjamin Thornigold. Without question, Thornigold gave Teach his earliest lessons in the use of terror as the most effective means of overwhelming a merchant ship on the high seas.

We first hear of Blackbeard as a pirate cruising with Thornigold in the West Indies. A short time later Thornigold and Teach sailed from New Providence for the American mainland, capturing several vessels in quick order. The prizes included a Bermuda wine pinky, a Havana sloop loaded with flour and a craft from Madeira with a rich cargo of silks and bullion.

Their next important capture was a large French Guineaman, on which the spoils were valuable, the men soft and the women plentiful. By this time Teach, an apt pupil of a fearsome master, had risen high in the estimation of his captain. Encouraged by his obvious approval, Teach boldly approached Thornigold one day and asked if he could become commander of the latest captured ship. Thornigold roared in pleasure at his protege's audacity, but nevertheless he shouted that Teach was getting too big for his breeches.

Teach had by now grown a horrible-looking black beard which, according to tradition, was more luxuriant than any other beard ever seen. It supposedly covered every inch of the pirate's face, growing up to his eyelids and hiding his ears. In fact, it is said that one couldn't tell where Teach's beard left off and his hair began. The pirate had let both grow extremely long to make himself more formidable and his victims more vulnerable.

Legend relates that when Thornigold finally gave his ambitious pupil command of a ship, the captain also bestowed upon him the name "Blackbeard," by which Teach was known until the end of his days.

When, a few years later, the British government issued offers of pardon to all pirates who would give up their profession, Captain Thornigold, who had a sizable amount of treasure laid away, sold his two vessels to Blackbeard and left the sea.

Blackbeard took the best ship, named her *Queen Anne's Revenge* and began a career of bloodthirsty conquest, pillage and murder never equaled in the annals of piracy. One of his memorable captures was near the isle of Saint Vincent, where he overcame the crew and passengers of the *Great Allan,* took all the supplies from her and burned and sank the ship. The men of the *Allan* who chose to join the pirates lived; the others were quickly massacred and their bodies thrown overboard.

Blackbeard next sailed for Bermuda. One dark night off the shores of the islands he noticed the lights of several vessels. In the morning he saw that they were three British sloops, and boarding them in turn, he killed every man aboard who would not join his pirate fleet and then took over the vessels and their cargoes.

The next day Blackbeard fell in with two French ships headed for Martinique, one without cargo and the other heavily loaded with sugar and cocoa. Teach murdered everyone aboard both vessels. He then sailed for the North

Carolina shore, where he soon got together with Governor Charles Eden of North Carolina, an official who never looked too closely into the background of a lucrative business arrangement. Blackbeard told Eden that he had found the captured ships adrift at sea and Eden accepted his explanation. They shared the profits and Blackbeard sailed away for more booty.

Blackbeard kept a diary of his exploits, though little of it has been preserved. I quote an excerpt:

Such a day, rum all out:—Our company somewhat sober: ... confusion amongst us! Rogues a-plotting;—Great talk of separation—so I look sharp for a prize:—Such a day, took one with a great deal of liquor aboard, so kept the company hot ... then all things went well again.

On April 9, 1717, Blackbeard's fleet reached the Bay of Honduras, where they overtook a ship and four sloops. When Blackbeard raised his famous pirate flag, the sailors fled ashore, for they knew what their fate would be if they were caught. The ship was the *Protestant Caesar* of Boston, commanded by Captain Wyar. Blackbeard, chagrined that the men had escaped, burned the ship to the water's edge. He had a special hatred for Boston vessels, for the residents of that port had the unmitigated nerve to hang pirates when they captured them.

Finally Blackbeard became such a menace to the ocean lanes that the British Navy decided that they had to capture him. The man-of-war *Scarborough,* carrying thirty guns, was sent in search of him. One moonlit night the *Queen Anne's Revenge* and the *Scarborough* sighted each other.

At dawn they came together. It was a long, hard-fought battle, with blood running into the scuppers of both ships, but Blackbeard, his men collapsing and dying all around him, would not surrender. The British captain ordered the *Scarborough* to retreat to the island of Barbados, and Blackbeard, licking his wounds, could now boast that he had defeated the Royal Navy. It was the first time in maritime history that such an event had occurred.

Teach now sailed in triumph for Spanish America, where his fame preceded him everywhere.

During his return trip, he fell in with a certain Major Stede Bonnet, a Southern gentleman who had adopted piracy as a relief from boredom. Bonnet knew nothing of navigation, and Blackbeard suggested that he join the crew of the *Queen Anne's Revenge.* Bonnet agreed to give up his own ship and go aboard Blackbeard's as a lieutenant.

A short time later Edward Teach decided to take advantage of the royal proclamation of clemency and went ashore at Ocracoke for several months. Then, tiring of his idleness on the island, he returned to his old profession.

His first capture after emerging from his retirement was in the Bay of Honduras, where he overtook the sloop *Adventure,* placing Israel Hands (whom many of you have read about in Stevenson's *Treasure Island*) aboard the *Adventure* as captain. Week after week passed with captures almost every day. Finally, Blackbeard took his fleet and headed north, accompanied by Major Bonnet, who by this time had learned enough navigation to become master of his own vessel again.

Arriving off the bar at Charleston, South Carolina,

Blackbeard captured five vessels in two days, practically closing the port of Charleston, for no sea captain would sail while Blackbeard was waiting off the bar to pounce on his ship. With more than two hundred prisoners crowded aboard his flagship, Teach then sent his lieutenant, Captain Richards, to Charleston with a demand for a chest of medicine for the pirate fleet. Teach could afford to be arrogant, for aboard his ship as one of the hostages was a prominent citizen of Charleston, Samuel Bragg, one of the governor's councilmen. Captain Richards and his two assistants strutted through the streets of Charleston as they awaited delivery of the medical supplies. Only when they had returned to the fleet with a giant chest of medicine worth over three hundred pounds did Blackbeard release all the prisoners.

There were many who referred to Blackbeard as the very devil himself. One night soon after his successful exploits at Charleston the pirate decided to give an exhibition of his Mephistophelean qualities. He took three of the more venturesome members of his crew aside, and, fixing his ferocious black eyes on them, told of his scheme. "Come," he roared, raising himself to his full height, "let us make a hell of our own and try how long we can bear it."

All four men descended into the hold. After Blackbeard had closed the hatches, he filled several large pots with brimstone and set them on fire. The four pirates remained in the hold, breathing the suffocating smoke into their lungs until all but Blackbeard shouted for air. Then he released the hatches and allowed the others to pull themselves up on deck, not a little pleased that he had held out longer than any of his men.

Next Blackbeard sailed to North Carolina, where he gave another demonstration of his own particular brand of wickedness. His ship was heavily loaded with gold and silver bullion and specie, so Blackbeard decided to "clean house" and reduce the number of his men entitled to a share in the division of the spoils.

There were four ships in his fleet at that time, Major Stede Bonnet having sailed away on another mission. Blackbeard ordered the smallest of the craft to stand by, had all the spoils removed to it, and then, on the pretense of having the other three vessels careened for cleaning, he ran them toward the shore. Immediately after the ships were stranded, Teach chose forty of his men and with them went aboard the tender, which he had kept aside, leaving more than three hundred men ashore near the careened vessels. Then he sailed off with his picked crew. He never saw the others again.

But even forty men, Blackbeard decided, was too large a number to share his loot with. Reaching an island several leagues away, where there was "neither bird nor beast nor herb," he sent ashore seventeen of his men, ostensibly to find a suitable place for burying some of his treasure. Once they were on land, Blackbeard hoisted anchor and sailed away, leaving the seventeen marooned on the desert isle. Going ashore on another island, he divided the spoils with the remainder of the crew, reduced by his cunning from almost four hundred to twenty-three. Luckily for the marooned men, Major Stede Bonnet heard about Blackbeard's act and rescued the pirates, allowing them to join his fleet, which was then gaining fame of its own.

Meanwhile, Teach had sailed for Bathtown, for an interview with his confederate, Governor Charles Eden of North Carolina. Teach told Eden that he had decided to retire from piracy again and wished for a pardon, which Eden as governor had the power to grant. Eden compliantly called together a Court of Vice-Admiralty. Its decision was a foregone conclusion and Edward Teach was adjudged an honest privateer again.

In North Carolina today you often hear the legend that Blackbeard fell in love with Governor Eden's daughter when he met her at the conclusion of one of his trips. Present-day historians point out the ruins of a brick tunnel which formerly ran from the water front to Governor Eden's home. This tunnel was believed to have been used by Blackbeard in bringing his piratical spoils into the governor's cellar. It is said that the girl surprised the pirate one night as he was superintending the storing of goods in the basement of her father's home and that Blackbeard desired her at first sight.

With the consent of Governor Eden, the story continues, Blackbeard paid court to his daughter. The girl loved another, a sea captain who at that time was on the way home from England, but Blackbeard would not accept her refusal. He planned to kidnap the girl and sail away with her. Governor Eden warned his daughter of Blackbeard's plans, and in the middle of the night, accompanied by a Mrs. Margaret Palmer, Miss Eden is supposed to have taken refuge in the Old Marsh House of Bathtown.

Foiled in his plans, Blackbeard put to sea at once and lay in wait for the girl's lover. He captured and killed the young captain, cut off his right hand and packed it in a small silver casket. This grisly package he had delivered to Miss Eden as though it were a costly present. Upon opening the casket the girl cried out in horror and fainted dead away. Within a month she died and Blackbeard's revenge was complete.

Actually the story, although worthy of Blackbeard, cannot possibly be true, for neither Miss Eden nor Mrs. Palmer was born until after Blackbeard's death, and the Old Marsh House was not built until 1744, over a quarter of a century after Blackbeard fought his last battle.

When Blackbeard was pardoned by Governor Eden's court, he acquired another woman as his wife and with her sailed north to the Isles of Shoals, off the New Hampshire coast. There he lived happily with his bride for several weeks while supposedly burying a substantial treasure of silver bars and coins on the two islands of Smuttynose and Londoner. Just as he finished his men reported a strong British fleet in the offing with one man-of-war, on its way to Londoner Island, and Blackbeard was forced to flee. Mrs. Blackbeard was left on Smuttynose Island to await the return of her husband.

Blackbeard never returned, however, and tradition tells us that the woman lived for many years at the Isles of Shoals, until her death in 1735. It is said that her ghost still haunts the lonely place.

Although he sailed away from the Isles of Shoals with

English ships in pursuit, Blackbeard managed to reach his favorite resting place, Ocracoke Island, without being captured. There he went ashore to meet his many wives and children again.

He was not idle for long, however. He soon took a short cruise, during which he decided to show the other pirates once more just how fiendish he could be. One evening as he was relaxing with his own men, sitting at table with his two trusty henchmen, Captain Israel Hands and Captain Richards, the latter saw a strange light in his leader's eyes. Then Blackbeard reached into his pocket and pulled out several fuses, which he began lighting and attaching to his hideous beard. This was his peculiar custom when he went into battle but he had never before adopted it under peaceful circumstances. The hint was enough for Richards, who fled to the deck above, but Hands had fallen asleep and had no idea of what was taking place.

Blackbeard now began to chuckle to himself and cocked two of the many pistols which he always carried. Then he gave a great bellow, awakening Hands.

"What's the trouble?" asked the sleepy pirate, blinking and rubbing his eyes. Blackbeard smiled diabolically across the table.

"There's no trouble," he replied. "We're just going to have a little fun. It's a new game I've made up." He drew in his breath, and at the same time held the guns under the table.

"Now," he shouted, blowing out the candles to leave the cabin in darkness, "here's something to remember me by!" In the blackness of the cabin, he crossed his arms and fired blindly under the table. Then he rushed up on deck, throwing the guns into the sea.

Israel Hands, badly wounded, was taken into his own quarters, and later carried ashore at Bathtown. When he recovered, the authorities placed him under arrest, for, unknown to the pirate, the forces of law and righteousness had finally united against Teach.

The British Government determined to destroy Blackbeard, for they had never forgotten his insult to the Royal Navy in forcing the *Scarborough* to retreat. The British took several decisive steps at this time, the first of which was to see that Blackbeard was properly condemned as a pirate. Because the Governor of North Carolina could not be trusted to take action against his friend and confederate, it was arranged that Governor Alexander Spotswood of Virginia should issue his own proclamation. On November 24, 1718, Governor Spotswood offered a reward of one hundred pounds for Blackbeard, and corresponding sums for each member of his crew or the crew of any other pirate vessel.

Now the British Navy put Captain Robert Maynard in charge of an expedition to capture Blackbeard. Captain Maynard chose two crews from the men-of-war *Pearl* and *Lime,* then at anchor in the James River, hired two small sloops capable of sailing over the shoals around Ocracoke and lost no time in getting his expedition ready for sea. Sailing from Kicquetan on the James River, the two vessels reached the mouth of Ocracoke Inlet, where the spars and masts of Blackbeard's vessel were sighted.

On Ocracoke, Blackbeard saw the two sloops approach-

ing and stripped his own vessel for action, but by the tim
Maynard had reached a point off Ocracoke Village, dark
ness had fallen and the British leader wisely decided t
anchor for the night. The channel was dangerous and th
shoals were many.

With the coming of dawn, Maynard sent a small boa
ahead to guide him towards Blackbeard's refuge, but i
spite of all precautions, the sloop grounded many times
To lighten the vessels, Maynard first ordered all the ballas
thrown overboard, and then he commanded that the wate
barrels be emptied. Finally, he approached within canno
shot of the enemy. Blackbeard opened the engagement b
firing a cannon ball, but it failed of its mark and hit th
water between the two sloops of the Royal Navy. Maynard
hoisted his King's Colors at once, whereupon Blackbeard
cut his anchor cable, planning to make a run for it if h
could.

Blackbeard had a tremendous advantage with twenty can
non aboard, but he did not realize that the sloops had
abandoned their heavy armament for the sake of greate
mobility. The lighter vessel, Maynard's sloop, was able to
slide over the shoal, but her companion ship maneuvered
against a sand bar and stuck fast. Deciding to get action,
even though he must do it alone, Maynard ordered his
sweeps put out. He rapidly closed the distance between his
sloop and the pirate ship.

Soon the two opponents were near enough for hailing,
and Edward Teach aimed his foghorn voice at the plucky
representative of the British Navy. "Who are you?" Blackbeard shouted. "And whence came you?"

"You may see from our colors we are no pirates," replied Maynard.

"Come aboard with your small boat!" suggested Blackbeard cannily. But the British captain was not to be caught.

"I cannot spare my boat, but I will come aboard of you as soon as I can with my sloop." This answer so upset the pirate that he rushed below for a quick drink of rum before continuing the conversation.

"Damnation seize my soul if I give you quarter or take any from you," the angered buccaneer roared.

Maynard's reply rang out across the water. "I don't expect quarter from you, nor shall I give any."

In spite of his bold words, Maynard knew that he was up against the strongest pirate in all the western seas, a brutal man with a staggering record of victorious battles and bloody captures. In maneuvering for a good position, Blackbeard's craft ran aground, giving the British hope for a successful approach. But the tide came in and freed the pirate vessel. Shortly afterwards the wind died down completely. Again resorting to his sweeps, for Maynard was afraid that his prey would escape, the British officer drew close to the notorious buccaneer.

Suddenly Teach, deciding that he would have to fight his way out, ordered his battery of guns made ready and gave the command to fire. It was a mighty broadside, and when the smoke died down twenty-nine of Maynard's men were either killed or wounded. Maynard ordered all survivors below and pretended that he, the helmsman and two sailors were the only ones aboard who were still alive.

Blackbeard, his spirits rising at his apparent success, drew closer.

"Look at 'em!" he shouted. 'Why, there's only three or four of 'em still alive! All the rest are knocked on the head. Let's jump aboard and cut the others to pieces! Let no one live to see sunset!"

And jump he did, with fourteen of his men. Maynard then signaled for his own sailors below to rush up on deck. The element of surprise made it an even fight, for Maynard had twelve men and Blackbeard fourteen.

Both captains spotted each other at the same moment and both fired instantly. Blackbeard missed fire with his first pistol and then again with his second. But Maynard had lodged a bullet in the pirate's leg. The buccaneer still had his cutlass, however, a mighty weapon which two ordinary men would have had difficulty in swinging. The opponents parried for a moment, and then Blackbeard brought his heavier blade down on the British officer's sword, snapping it off at the hilt.

"Now I've got you!" shouted the triumphant pirate. But he had spoken too soon, for just as he drew back for his final thrust, an alert British marine stabbed him in the throat.

Howling like a wounded beast, Blackbeard turned against his new attacker, but he was soon hemmed in on all sides. On and on he fought with cutlass and pistol, until he was bleeding from twenty saber thrusts and five gun wounds. Bending over to fire once more, Blackbeard was seized with a terrible convulsion and tottered for a moment in helplessness. His cutlass and pistol clattered to the deck. Then

e mighty pirate dropped dead before the man who had
vorn to capture him, Robert Maynard of the Royal Navy.

By this time Maynard's other sloop had arrived on the
ene and her crew boarded the pirate vessel on the oppo-
te side. The marines rushed below just in time to prevent
e explosion of Blackbeard's ship, for they caught a giant
Negro about to throw a blazing torch into an open powder
arrel. The Negro and the remaining pirates surrendered.

Before sailing away from Ocracoke, Captain Maynard
imself boarded the pirate ship and went into Blackbeard's
bin, where he found many letters and papers, among
em incriminating correspondence between Governor
den, the Governor's collector, the secretary to the Gov-
nor and Blackbeard. There was other correspondence
ith certain traders from New York, but the Eden letters
ere particularly incriminating. No wonder the Negro
ewman had tried to blow up the ship!

With this irrefutable evidence on hand, Captain Maynard
rdered Teach's head severed from his body and suspended
om the bowsprit of the victorious sloop, and the British
essel sailed into Bathtown, displaying this grisly emblem
f victory.

Respecting no authority, when Maynard reached Bath-
own he took a squad of men to the Governor's storehouse.
Here he ripped open the doors and discovered eighty hogs-
eads of sugar, sixty of them belonging to the Governor
nd twenty to his secretary, Mr. Knight. The eighty bar-
els for Eden and Knight had been declared by Blackbeard
s their part of the booty in a recent capture. Although Gov-
rnor Eden managed to weather the storm of adverse pub-

lic opinion, his secretary, made of weaker material, fel
sick with the "fright," and died within a few days of th
shameful discovery.

Fourteen of the captured pirates were hanged a shor
time later; a few of the remainder were pardoned. Amon
those pardoned was Israel Hands, Stevenson's character i
Treasure Island, who was allowed to sail back to England
where he occupied himself as a professional beggar fo
many years.

What happened to the fabulous Blackbeard treasure?

There are two important incidents which would indi
cate the possibility that Blackbeard did bury treasure at th
Isles of Shoals. The first occurred some time before 1820
when Captain Samuel Haley of Smuttynose Island uncov
ered five bars of silver on the shore. After realizing $3000
from the sale of the silver, he devoted some of the money
from his unexpected find toward building a breakwater
across to Malaga Island.

The second incident took place during World War II
At the height of the conflict several government representa
tives went ashore on Londoner Island, where they made
some interesting discoveries. Mrs. Prudence Randall
daughter of the Reverend Frank B. Crandall, owner of
Londoner Island, told me the following story about their
visit.

Government men who went ashore on our island without per-
mission found definite indications that there was a substantia
amount of silver still buried on the landing side of the beach

acing the Star Island Hotel. The exact location is about halfway across the half-moon stretch of the beach.

We have been told that Blackbeard buried his loot here. He buried silver bars on our island and his crew buried some silver bars and a considerable quantity of pieces of eight over on Smuttynose. Captain Haley found the silver bars on Smuttynose Island but never found the pieces of eight. The remainder of that treasure is just below the water line on the beach east of the breakwater at Smuttynose.

We were told that our silver bars, probably worth thousands of dollars, are so far down in the sand that it would be a very costly experiment to locate them and bring them to the surface. Actually I have been within a few feet of their location.

Both my father and I agree that there is no doubt that the treasure is still buried down in the sand between the high and low water marks. Yes, we'll share fifty-fifty with any ambitious person who cares to search for it, after they have our permission in writing to land on the island.

The sand shifts so rapidly out there after every storm that, whereas you might know where to look one week, why the next week everything would be changed. But the silver doesn't move much, as it is too heavy, and it's there, waiting for someone with money and a feeling for adventure to go after it. The government men gave it up, saying that it would take several thousands of dollars for dredges and pumps.

Prudence Randall

Did Blackbeard himself leave any clues as to where his treasure was buried? It is said that on the eve of his last battle, one of Teach's henchmen questioned him about it. The pirate's reply was typical: "Nobody but the Devil and

myself know where my treasure is, and the longer liver of
the two shall have it all."

Teach died as he had lived. One of the most ferocious
pirates of all times, he ended his career as he probably would
have chosen, fighting a worthy opponent in the throes of
a struggle to the death.

Although, in general, the last of Blackbeard's mortal re
mains have long been considered to have crumbled to dust
such is not the case. When his head was brought into Bath
town after his death, it was obtained by one of the influ
ential men of the town, who had the skull lined with silver
inside and out, after which the bolder members of the
family would challenge each other to drink toasts from
it. Later it became the property of one of the members of
a college fraternity, who had it resilvered, and initiation
were instituted whereby any person who wished to qualify
for the fraternity would have to drink a pint of wine from
Blackbeard's skull.

When the fraternity dissolved about the time of the
American Revolution the skull was reclaimed by its owner
who then bought a tavern on the Potomac River. At his
death his son continued the tavern, and exhibited the skull
from time to time.

Between the years 1797 and 1811 John Bernard, who
wrote of his travels around America, recorded his impres
sions of a visit to the tavern. His writings were published
in 1886 with the title, *Retrospections of America,* from
which I quote the following:

"we spent our time in fishing-excursions to the Potomac, fre quently dining at a tavern on its banks. Here a drinking-vessel supposed to give a particular zest to punch was a skull tipped with silver, said to be a relic of the celebrated pirate Teach, or 'Blackbeard.' "

Bernard then went on to describe the pirate battle already included in this chapter, ending his remarks by explaining how the victor "with the next stroke severed the pirate's black head from his shoulders. He then ordered it to be put in boiling water and thoroughly cleansed, when he took it on shore and made it a present to the progenitor of its present possessor."

In the year 1949 I visited Alexandria and called at the residence of ninety-one-year-old William Buckner Mc-Groarty, Virginia historian, to discuss research I was conducting about a mystery at Gadsby's tavern there. During my interview with him, a chance remark involving Blackbeard led to my later discovery of the infamous pirate's venerable skull in a nearby section of Virginia, still with its silvered coating. After considerable discussion, examination, and appraisal, the skull became my property.

But the fabled treasure of Blackbeard is still being sought. In the summer of 1939, three Portsmouth youths, using a discarded navy craft and a second-hand diving suit, explored the bottom around the Isles of Shoals. They were Autus Williams, nineteen, George Williams, eighteen, both sons of Navy Diver Mendarus Williams of Rye Beach, and Ernest Morris, eighteen, also of Rye Beach. Although they did find wreckage of other craft, they didn't discover Blackbeard's treasure.

Late in the year 1950, many New England papers carried the news that a treasure-seeking company was on location at the Isles of Shoals. The group had already made arrangements for a local bank to keep open day and night to receive a large treasure, which was soon to be found. Allegedly, the treasure had been located from an airplane by a photographer who had equipped his camera with a special new-type film which was so sensitive that it would react to the presence of gold and silver buried on the island. When the photographer developed the film, there was the evidence that treasure was on the island! I merely offer this summary of the latest Isles of Shoals treasure hunt story without any attempt to explain it or indicate my opinion one way or another. Nothing has been heard recently of the organization's efforts.

Some day some one may find a substantial portion of the great hoard which Blackbeard buried, but I doubt it. Perhaps the best comment on the treasure was made by the pirate himself, when he stated that only he and the devil knew where it was buried.

CHAPTER 8

The Byfield Buccaneers

THE story of the Byfield Buccaneers, which is possibly so-titled because the men involved were neither buccaneers nor from Byfield, is so interwoven with local traditions and beliefs that it is an almost impossible task to separate the misleading stories and legends from the facts. It was only after many trips in and around Newburyport, Byfield and Georgetown, Massachusetts, that I was able to piece together the many scattered fragments of as interesting a treasure story as one could hope for.

In several cases information was given me reluctantly and only after I had promised not to reveal the names and addresses of those who helped me discover certain details of the story, but I have been permitted to include the names of Orin A. Arlin and Fred Dudley Pearson of Byfield, who both proved extremely helpful, and that of Miss Grace Bixby of the Newburyport Public Library, who did research work in the old records for me. Mr. Frederick E. Green strongly questioned certain aspects of the story, as he had been unable to find supporting evidence in the newspapers and records of the day.

Our actual tale begins far from Newburyport, down in the West Indies. Captain Roger Hayman, renegade Englishman, was in command of a pirate stronghold which operated with its headquarters at the western end of the Island of Haiti. Hayman had even attacked United States men-of-war when they were becalmed in the Gulf of Gonaive, and the pirates simply overwhelmed merchantmen caught in the vicinity.

Late in December, 1799, in an effort to halt the depredations of Captain Hayman, the United States sent a small fleet into the area, and the U. S. armed schooner, *Experiment,* commanded by Lieutenant William Maley, was ordered to convoy four merchantmen by the Island of Haiti.

On January 1, 1800, a dead calm set in, and sure enough, Captain Hayman decided to attack. Soon ten barges, each manned by from forty to fifty pirates, set out from Haiti, with Captain Hayman in command of the flotilla. They caught up with the becalmed convoy off the Island of Gonaive, and the navy schooner was unable to protect all four ships at once. Hayman started for two of the ships, whose crews fled shoreward at his approach. He first boarded an American merchantman, from which he removed the strongbox, and then quickly went aboard the one English vessel of the convoy, taking off with him her purser's chest of British sovereigns.

But before Captain Hayman could get ashore the *Experiment* caught up with him, and, in a brisk exchange of gunfire, sank three of the barges and killed a great number of the pirates. Captain Hayman himself was seriously wounded, while aboard the American vessel one man was killed and two were injured. A short time later the frigate *Boston* fell in with the pirates and in the course of a running fight with them, disabled five more of the pirate barges.

The pages of the *Massachusetts Spy* for March 5, May 7, and August 20, 1800, give all the details of this stirring battle, which was fought off the Island of Gonaive, but few Newburyport citizens realized that it would have lasting repercussions in nearby Byfield.

Keeping the two chests which he had captured in the recent fight, Hayman divided the remainder of his spoils amongst his followers, after which he "acquired" a trim schooner of 295 tons. He then sailed away from his pirate stronghold and crossed the ocean, landing at Liverpool more dead than alive, for his battle wounds were slowly killing him.

Selling the schooner, Hayman dispersed his crew with the exception of his four most faithful henchmen. He had left Liverpool eight years before, and was planning to return to his family there, but found that they had emigrated to New York. Anxious to follow them, he made arrangements to sail across the ocean again, in spite of the warning of a Liverpool physician that he should not attempt the trip.

Hayman engaged passage on the same brig which was to carry a certain Doctor Griffin to the New World. The young physician had become involved in certain unsavory activities which are better left unmentioned, and his family thought it best that he move to America, where the stigma of his disgrace might be forgotten with the passing of the years.

Nineteen hours before the scheduled sailing, Dr. Griffin was standing on the quarter-deck when an unusual event took place. The brig's purser appeared in the company of Captain Hayman, who was in turn followed by his four loyal henchmen carrying two heavy chests. All six men came aboard, and Griffin soon heard the heavy triple-studded door of the purser's cabin thrown open. He glanced down through the skylight just in time to see the men vanish inside with the chests. Ten minutes later Griffin watched as farewells were said between Hayman and his men. The four then left the vessel.

The brig sailed on schedule with the tide the next day, and all went well aboard for several weeks. Then, early one morning, there came a tap on Dr. Griffin's door. It was the purser.

"I've a very sick man for you," he began, "and I'd appreciate it if you could come at once." Five minutes later Griffin was standing at the bunk of Captain Hayman. Indeed the sailor was extremely ill, as the doctor's inspection revealed.

"There isn't much that I can do," he whispered to the purser, "for the patient is very low. Why he went to sea in his condition is a mystery. His death is only a few weeks or a month away at best." A strange expression came over the face of the purser, but just at that moment the sick man opened his eyes and looked up.

"Don't forget your promise," he whispered to the purser.

Two weeks later the purser again knocked on Griffin's door, and was invited in. "I suppose that you've been wondering just what Hayman meant when he told me not to forget my promise," he said.

"Why, yes, I've been wondering, but it's none of my business."

"Well, that may be, but I need help. There are two treasures in my strongbox which he had brought aboard. Hayman is an Englishman by birth, but he was actually a West Indian pirate. Hayman reached Liverpool with a hoard of money just two months ago, to find that his family had gone to New York. He wrote them that he was coming. Now here's where you come in. You tell me Hayman is too sick to realize what's going on, and can't live long. Well, I'm going to forget his family and keep the treasure, and there's ten percent in it for you if you help out."

And so it was arranged that the purser and Doctor Griffin should remove the treasure upon their arrival in New York.

But Griffin got to thinking about it one night. One of his friends aboard, Stearns Compton by name, was traveling to New York. They met each other outside the small stateroom which served as a social parlor. As they swung open the door another passenger was playing the piano which stood against the starboard bulkhead. That suited Griffin's plans, for then they would not be overheard. He told Compton the entire story from beginning to end.

"You know," he concluded, "that Purser Hanson never will be able to carry out his plan, for pirate Hayman has written to his family and they'll surely be at the New York pier awaiting him. Besides, if Hanson's going to take it from Hayman's family, we can just as well take it from him.

"Now here's what I propose to do. Newburyport, our first stop, is about ten days away. There the brig discharges a small part of her cargo before going on to New York. The purser will have to go ashore on company business, and he thinks that I am to stay aboard until we reach New York. As for Hayman, he's too weak to know what's going on.

"We'll arrange so that I'll go ashore and get a horse and shay, while you unlock the strong box with the extra key which I obtained. You pack the gold and silver into canvas bags and repack them into my sea chest. We'll get it loaded aboard the shay and start overland. How about it?"

"What have I to lose?" came the answer, and thus the bargain was sealed. Each man signed a statement to share and share alike, and then they left the cabin.

Nine days later the brig arrived in Newburyport Harbor and was soon warped into her pier. Every man who could went ashore, for they had been over a month at sea.

Soon only Griffin, Compton, and the sick man were left aboard. After signaling to Compton to go into the purser's quarters and start packing the money, Griffin disappeared. Within an hour Compton had opened the mariner's chests, transferred the gold and silver to the canvas money bags, and repacked them in Griffin's trunk, which he wrapped in canvas.

Fifteen minutes later the door swung open. Griffin stood there on the threshold, strangely elated, his cheeks burning with excitement.

"Is it here?"

"Yes."

"Did anyone else come back?"

"No."

"Well, let's hurry." Griffin stepped outside and held up his hand. Instantly two men appeared, entered the cabin, and placed a small platform with four handles under the trunk. Getting help from both Griffin and Compton, they raised it with great effort. Soon they were out on deck and down the gangway.

Reaching the horse and shay, they loaded the sea chest into the back of the vehicle, were paid off, and vanished into the night.

Griffin jumped into the carriage and seized the reins. Compton was soon beside him.

"I know the way," Griffin told his companion. "We'll keep on this road."

Two hours later they had reached a small inn or tavern by the side of the highway, in the parish of Byfield, known as the Pearson Tavern.

It was at this tavern that eccentric Lord Timothy Dexter used to visit. The inn was run at that time by Jeremiah Pearson, the great-great-grandfather of Fred Dudley Pearson, whom I mentioned earlier in this chapter. Jeremiah Pearson agreed to give Griffin and Compton lodging for the night. Pearson retired shortly afterwards, but, unknown to him, the two men took turns all night long in watching the barn where the treasure was concealed, to make sure it was safe.

Morning finally came at the Pearson Inn and Jeremiah Pearson gave the travelers a good breakfast before they started out. They were about to leave when a man on horseback rode up.

"Have you heard the latest?" he queried Pearson. "Two men escaped from a brig in Newburyport Harbor with the purser's money. We hear that they are on their way to Boston."

And with that final remark the horseman galloped away into the morning sunlight.

"Gentlemen," Pearson asked, "whence came you last night?"

"From Haverhill," Griffin replied promptly, but he decided to leave as soon as possible.

The two paid their bill and drove away, taking the Andover Road until they reached the Parker River, where they stopped, determined to bury the money. Unknown to them, however, a boy, Howard Noyes by name, had climbed a tree in the vicinity to observe some birds in a nest and happened to glance across and see the men when they got out of the shay near that point.

Taking the canvas wrapping from their treasure chest, they laboriously carried the coin to a point within sight of a large boulder of trap granite, on which Griffin began to pound out with hammer and chisel the letter "A," six inches high, as a marker. Meanwhile, Compton started to dig a hole with a small spade and soon had a pit four feet deep. The money was quickly piled into the hole, and the dirt and foliage was smoothed over the top again.

High in the tree, young Noyes became frightened by this time. He climbed down and fled home, where he told his story, but a search of the area failed to reveal either the freshly-dug earth or the treasure—although the letter "A" was plain to see on the granite boulder.

Meanwhile, the two schemers reached Boston, abandoned their vehicle, and took the stage for New York. Parting in the city, they agreed to return and dig up the treasure in five years.

But in five years much can happen, and each man prospered in his chosen profession. When the given time had elapsed, they decided by mutual consent against the risk of returning to Byfield. The years went by and still they did not go to collect the loot. They learned later that the pirate had died the day before the brig reached New York, and that the purser had told the police only those details which he had chosen to reveal.

Neither man ever returned to Byfield and both were dead by 1857. Sixty-six years later, a great-granddaughter of Compton inherited the strange pact concerning the treasure which the two men had signed. Compton had sealed it in an envelope with information about where he had buried the treasure, and each generation of his descendants had unsealed the envelope, read the instructions and done nothing but reseal the envelope. They wanted no part of the disgraceful matter.

But this particular lady, Compton's great-granddaughter,

became fascinated by the document, and wrote to the Pearson Tavern, where Fred Dudley Pearson was living. She thought that she would be revealing unknown information.

But, of course, almost half the residents of Byfield had heard the story before, because of young Howard Noyes, who had watched the treasure burial from high in the tree. Excitement developed again after the arrival of the letter from Compton's great-granddaughter and many more holes were dug. However, although in all over a hundred attempts were made in the vicinity, the treasure had not been discovered as late as 1932.

About nineteen years ago a certain workman was digging a well not too great a distance from the rock marked "A."

Orin A. Arlin visited the scene and spoke to him. "How are you coming with the well?" he asked.

"No water yet," came the short reply.

Late the following afternoon, Orin returned. The workman had vanished, and there were indications that he had discovered something very unusual. Old oak splinters and fragments of canvas lay strewn at the bottom of the well hole, and everything pointed to a hasty exit on the laborer's part.

Arlin never saw the well-digger again, but one day when he was over at a store on Ring's Island, Salisbury, the proprietor spoke up:

"Say, Orin, your friend, the well-digger, was in the other day, and look what he used for money to pay for his purchases!"

The merchant held up a handful of silver dollars, still

fairly bright and shiny, except for some badly tarnished places. Orin Arlin told me about it later in detail.

"I saw the dates on those coins, and obtained several for myself. The dates ranged from 1794 to 1799, the years just previous to the time when the chests full of silver dollars were taken from the two merchant ships by Captain Hayman. Although my friend, the well-digger, told Pete that he got the money by winning a lottery, I believe that he really blundered onto the old hidden treasure, or at least a part of it!"

Mr. Arlin later gave me one of the silver dollars, and it has a valued place in my collection of pirate skulls, skeletons, guns, and treasure, for I know the thrilling, bloody past with which the dollar is associated.

So now, after almost a century and a half, the Byfield treasure has appeared, or at least a part of it has, for the rest of British sovereigns, reputedly worth $70,000, have evidently never been found. Probably they still remain buried not too far from a rock marked "A," which is pointed out to visitors as they wander along the banks of the beautiful Parker River, in Byfield, Massachusetts.

CHAPTER 9

She Wore a Purple Cloak

TREASURE has been discovered in Winthrop, Massachusetts, on at least three occasions—in 1829, 1880, and 1887. Strangely enough, almost all of the discoveries are said to be connected with a woman in a purple cloak who appeared suddenly in Winthrop in 1868. Acting in a mysterious fashion, she accurately told of treasure found in the past and treasure which would be found in the future. The details concerning this unusual woman will be given later in this chapter.

At the end of the nineteenth century there were many residents of Winthrop who believed that the famous privateer, Captain William Kidd, buried treasure on Winthrop Beach, near the base of Great Head.

According to the Boston *Post* for March 29, 1896, Captain Kidd landed at Winthrop Beach in 1699, and his men seized several pigs belonging to the farm of one John Allen, after which they tied up Allen and his "strapping son." Kidd found this out and not only had the men cut the Allens loose, but also paid for the pigs in Spanish gold dollars.

The story goes that Privateer Kidd then sailed away. In 1701 came the news that William Kidd had been hanged as a murderer on the English gallows. From that day on the Allens dug for the treasure which they believed Captain Kidd must have buried on the beach at Winthrop, but no one ever found it. Incidentally, a ship loaded with silver was wrecked off Winthrop Beach in 1682, seventeen years before Kidd was hanged, and that particular treasure has never been recovered.

Late in the afternoon of March 6, 1829, Captain William Tewksbury, the famous lifesaver, arrived in Boston from Deer Island, located in Boston Harbor, with the news that Captain Savage and his entire crew had been lost on the *Elizabeth and Ann,* which was then coming ashore a shattered wreck, after hitting the rocks off Nahant during a storm. Her cargo of oranges and cigars was strewn all along the waterfront, from what is now Winthrop Highlands to the end of Deer Island. The captain's watch was found still hanging on a hook in the cabin which came up with other wreckage on the Point Shirley beach. The quarter deck washed ashore at Cedar Island at the entrance to Shirley Gut.

The day after the storm the inmates of the poorhouse

in Chelsea, along with several laborers, were gathering kelp and seaweed on the rocks near what is now Fort Heath, Winthrop. One young Negro lad, more active than the others, saw a partially submerged plank floating in waist-deep water. There seemed to be a white cloth attached to the wood, so he waded out into the water to get the plank.

To his astonishment, the boy found that the cloth was actually a large canvas bag, torn at one end. He could not easily lift it, but managed to bring it ashore. Pulling it up on the rocks, he opened the sack and found it was filled with gold pieces! The others naturally crowded around him, but the overseer was firm, and allowed the boy to keep his discovery for himself, taking him at once to the local Chelsea Bank. The money totaled a handsome fortune. Needless to say, the Negro's days as a poor-house laborer were over, but it would be most interesting to know just how much money he recovered and his subsequent life history.

Incidentally, the hole in the canvas bag had evidently allowed many of the gold coins to escape into the ocean. A search was made at the time, but nothing was found. Years later, around 1880, while the son of the Reverend Mr. Duffield was playing in the sand between Short Beach and Grover's Cliff, Winthrop, he dug up a coin with his shovel. Taking it to his father, the boy found that he was the happy owner of a gold piece. Word quickly traveled around, as news of that sort does, and soon the entire shoreline was crowded with people searching for gold pieces. Many of them were lucky, as the local papers of the period reported the finding of around three hundred dollars worth.

Whether more money is still unfound from the wreck of the *Elizabeth and Ann,* lost back in 1829, is an interesting question.

Another treasure story about Winthrop concerns that section of the town known as Point Shirley. In the month of October, 1868, omnibus carriages were still running to Point Shirley from Maverick Square, East Boston. From the last coach, which arrived in Point Shirley at about five in the afternoon, a woman dressed in a peculiar costume alighted from the omnibus. Besides her old-fashioned garments, she wore a long-flowing purple cloak.

A young boy, Wallace Wyman, watched the stranger climbing down from the stage. As he leaned against the rail fence on his father's farm, he wondered why the woman had arrived at Point Shirley so late in the day. The stagecoach on which she had come was now starting back for Boston and there would be no other until the next day.

Now the strange woman in purple advanced slowly up the hill to the place where Wallace Wyman was standing. "Young man, is this Point Shirley?" she asked.

"Yes, my lady, it is."

The woman studied the boy carefully before she continued. "Then I have come to the right location. You look like an honest lad, so I'll tell you why I am here. Last night I had a dream, a very vivid one, in fact, and I dreamed that I was standing at an old fort on a hill. Then there was a strange voice which kept repeating over and over to me . . . 'You are at the old fort at Pullen Point. . . . There is treasure all around you, especially to the north, east, south, and under your very feet.'

"Young man, that dream was so real that when I woke I couldn't believe I had been dreaming. I couldn't sleep any more that night, so I dressed and went down to the library, where I opened several books on Boston. Finally I found one which mentioned Pullen Point, and it said that the location was now known as Point Shirley. I was determined to go there. The idea obsessed me.

"Even then, as I live in Dorchester, it was quite a journey. Finally, by two o'clock, I had crossed the penny ferry at the foot of Hanover Street in Boston and arrived in East Boston, at Maverick Square, where I took the next stage to Point Shirley. Now I want to know if there is an old fort here and if so, where I will find it."

"Yes, there's a fort. It's on top of the hill, and the old stones which formed the foundation of the fort are still there."

"The stones are there? Why, I saw them in my dream, piled one above the other. Take me there at once, my lad."

Ten minutes later the Lady in the Purple Cloak and young Wallace Wyman arrived at the old stone fort, which had been at the top of Point Shirley Hill since the days of the American Revolution.

"Yes," began the mysterious Lady in the Purple Cloak, "this is the exact location of my dream. It all comes back to me now. There is treasure in the ground on which we stand, my lad. Make no mistake about that. And there is more treasure over on the island in front of us, and also on the island behind it. Then there is more treasure up there to the north, behind that high promontory. I know that I won't ever find any treasure, but I am passing the

information on to you, my lad. Some day, if you are indus-
trious, you'll find a fortune on this hill."

Just then she was interrupted by a high-pitched voice
calling, "Wallace, Wallace! Come to supper."

"That's my ma," cried Wallace, "and I'll have to go now."

He ran down the hill and disappeared into the house.
After supper he came out again, although by this time it
had grown quite dark, and he walked up to the old fort.
The Lady in the Purple Cloak had vanished. He searched
all over Point Shirley, but never again did he see the woman
who had arrived on the last stagecoach that evening. There
was no way she could have left Point Shirley except on
foot, and surely the woman could not walk six long miles
to Maverick Square at that time of night.

During the following days, Wallace often wondered what
could have happened to her, but he never learned. He did,
however, go up to the top of the hill and dig here and
there for the treasure which she had said was buried nearby.
But he soon gave up and after a few years nearly forgot the
entire incident.

Wallace Wyman grew to manhood and became a fisherman. One morning in 1887, when he was in his thirties, he
arose early to go out and haul his traps. After pulling on his
heavy rubber boots, he walked down to the back shore,
pushed his rowboat into the water and soon reached his
anchorage. While slipping his moorings, he noticed three
strangers leaving a schooner anchored in the offing. They
rowed ashore with a firm stroke and passed within fifty
yards of him on his way to the beach, where they landed a
quarter of a mile north of the old salt works.

As he hoisted sail on his own craft, he noticed that the men had shovels and picks with them. They soon pulled their skiff up above the reach of the incoming tide, and then struck off at a rapid clip toward the old Point Shirley fort.

Wallace Wyman thought no more of it and sailed out of the harbor to haul his traps. Late that afternoon, when he finished his work, the wind had died down and stranded him near Great Brewster Island. He realized that he was in for a long scull home. It was after dark when he finally neared Point Shirley. He noticed, however, that the strange schooner was still at anchor in the offing and that the dingy was alongside.

"Here's a chance to find out who those men are," Wyman thought to himself, and he sculled up slowly to the side of the schooner. Glancing through a porthole, he saw the three men, with guns drawn, sitting around an ancient, rust-covered sea chest, which was literally filled to the brim with gold and silver coins.

"They'll shoot me first and ask questions later," Wyman thought in horror. Just before he pushed off from the schooner, he heard one of the men mutter to the others, "The treasure of Long Ben Avery, after a hundred and fifty years!"

Wyman sculled silently off into the night. After going home and eating his supper, he took a lantern and climbed to the old fort. In the exact spot where he and the Lady in the Purple Cloak had stood years before, there was a yawning pit. He climbed down to investigate further, and at the bottom of the pit saw the outline of a chest, about fourteen inches long and eight inches wide, with the rust from the hinges still clinging to the dirt. At this sight, Wyman bitterly realized that untold riches had been within his grasp all his life.

Later, when the old pilothouse of the ship *Columbia* was stripped for metal, Wyman acquired it, sailed it across to Point Shirley, set it up near the beach as his home, and settled down to live comfortably in it by himself. The years passed uneventfully. By the 1930's Wyman was a man in his seventies, vigorous and active. He still lived in the pilothouse of the old *Columbia,* but Point Shirley had become a thriving community in the meantime, and the old building was by then hemmed in with modern dwellings. It was here that I found him in 1936, when I was collecting material for my history of Winthrop.

Some of the most interesting evenings of my entire life were those I spent at the old Point Shirley pilothouse. One night Wyman told me the story you have just read. And he told me, too, that treasure has actually been found in each of the places mentioned by the Lady in the Purple Cloak!

To tell all the stories about the various treasures mentioned by this elusive woman in purple, I shall include two more treasure stories in this chapter. A glance at the map will show what relationship Point Shirley has with the area nearby.

To the northward I have indicated Grover's Cliff, at Winthrop Highlands, where in 1880 a substantial sum was found. The two other islands mentioned to Wallace Wyman that night were Deer Island, and Lovell's Island, both marked on the map.

Deer Island has always been known as the island where buried treasure lies waiting for the lucky finder. Back in

the year 1819, Frederick William Augustus Steuben Brown, the wandering poet of Boston Bay, published his book on Boston Harbor and all its islands. About Deer Island he had the following to say:

Here superstition often tells,
  Of a ghost that's heard to screech,
And utter dismal piercing yells,
  At midnight on the beach.

For oft I've heard the story told,
  How a ghost without a head;
Here guards some thousand pounds in gold,
  By some strange fancy led.

In 1824, five years after this book of poems was published, three men hunted treasure down near Money Bluff, on the island. Captain William Tewksbury, celebrated life-saver of Boston; Brown the poet; and a Captain Crocker, dug silently in a spot where treasure was said to be located. Finally they gave up—and Crocker blamed the expedition's failure on the fact that one of them had spoken after promising to keep silent!

Years passed without any further attempt to find the "thousand pounds" which the headless ghost guards. Then, when a new reinforcement of the island was planned, with a sea wall, amazing things began to happen.

On Wednesday, October 17, 1906, lunch hour came for a group of government workmen building the new sea wall at Deer Island. One of them, Thomas Mahoney, perhaps more adventuresome than the others, decided to take a walk down on the shore before his lunch hour ended, and reached the water's edge. It was then low tide, and as he strode across the stony beach, his eye caught a sliver of metal shaped in the form of a disc. Picking it up, he examined it casually, and decided to keep it. It was such a blackened and discolored object that he paid no attention to it until late that afternoon, when he and the other engineers were waiting for the Deer Island Ferry to take them across to the mainland. He decided to tell his engineer friend, old John Andrews, about his discovery.

"Say, John," he began, "I've found something interesting down on the beach, and here it is!" The two men bent closely over the metal object, and examined it with care.

"Here, let me scrape some of that grime away," volunteered Andrews, and pulled out his knife. A few moments later he had removed the outer crust to such an extent that both men could see that it was a silver coin. That night Mahoney worked on the coin until he had exposed the markings entirely, to reveal the date, 1835, and the nationality of the coin as Mexican.

Returning with the other government engineers the next morning, he showed the coin around, and there was little lunch eaten that day when the men had finished their morning work on the sea wall.

A concerted rush for the beach began but only Mahoney knew where to look, of course. Unfortunately for the workers, the twenty-four hours had brought almost an hour's difference in the time of low tide, so the waters were almost covering the area where Mahoney had found the coin, and by the time the tide had gone out enough for a good search, the lunch hour ended.

The following day was even worse, but several of the men agreed to stay after work that afternoon and search by the light of a lantern, since the tide would be dead low around

dusk. Inspector Harry C. Rideout, in charge of the sea wall
project, allowed the men to carry out their plan.

Besides the two already mentioned, James Doherty, John
Higgins, Jack Olson and John Cunningham were interested
in searching further. The moment their work ended, they
went down on the beach and hunted for treasure, lighting
a lantern and continuing their efforts until the incoming tide
later that night prevented further work.

No less than two hundred coins were uncovered by this
band of searchers in the three hours that they hunted, and
when they reached the Shirley Gut Ferry, their discoveries
electrified the island. Most of the coins found were Mexican
silver dollars, but there were a goodly number of smaller
coins, including several gold pieces.

A few days later an account of the discovery appeared in
the *Boston Herald,* with a picture of Money Bluff. During
the following week no less than three hundred additional
coins were uncovered and salvaged, together with several
rusted pieces of iron, a few hinges, and an old padlock. A
fifteen-pound ring bolt was then spotted farther down the
beach.

The work on the sea wall continued, the men going down
on the beach from time to time when the tide was low and
finding coins. Then, with the coming of December, the
project was given up until spring. Estimates of the number
of coins and their value vary, of course, ranging from 550
coins worth $700 to 1200 coins worth $2,000.

Of all those who found the treasure coins on the Deer
Island shore, only one man still remains at Deer Island today. He is Engineer Frank Black, in charge of the Deer

Island Pumping Station. A boy when he found his share of the wealth, Black recalls that Lighthouse Keeper Pingree and Engineer Eric Swenson also found several of the coins.

"I've got the coins I found tucked away in the house somewhere," Black told me in February, 1951, "and my dates were in the 1850's. Some day I'll dig them out for you. But those who say that the treasure was found down near Money Bluff are wrong. That treasure was found near a great rock, which can still be seen at the end of the sea wall which is at the base of the hill near the radar tower. We'd all go over and search in the sand and clay around the vicinity of the giant rock."

Regardless of how much money actually was found, the treasure discovered in 1906 could never have been a part of the treasure said to have been buried out on Money Bluff and described in a poem written in 1819, long before the coins found in 1906 were even minted. So we must assume that the "ghost without a head" is still guarding her own particular treasure hoard! But what always puzzled Wallace Wyman was how his Lady in the Purple Cloak was so accurate in her statements as to where treasure would be found.

An incident which occurred in 1941 at Fort Dawes, on the island, might indicate to some that the famous ghost of Deer Island was still active. One stormy night, two officers were alone in their separate quarters at the fort. As midnight approached, the gale grew worse. The waves could be heard smashing against the beach on the harbor side of the island. Suddenly, above the noise of the storm, piercing screams echoed from the shore. Each officer, unknown to the other, started outdoors in the general direction of the cries. Meet-

ng on the beach, they searched the fort for a considerable
ime, but finally gave up the attempt and returned to their
ooms. Eventually it was agreed that the screams had come
rom the ghost who is "heard to screech and utter dismal
iercing yells, at midnight on the beach."

My personal opinion of the treasure found in 1906 is that
t was from the wreck of the schooner *Juliet,* lost on Fawn
3ar, January 9, 1886. Heavily coated with ice, the *Juliet*
vent over on her beam ends, and three men were drowned.
The other three were saved by volunteers from Deer Island.
Every schooner in those days carried a money chest for ex-
enses and the purchase of cargoes. Probably the coins came
rom the money chest of the ill-fated *Juliet.*

The last location of treasure mentioned by the woman
who wore the purple cloak was Lovell's Island, shown on
he map. Less than a mile from Deer Island, it has been
he scene of countless shipwrecks down through the years.
Perhaps the most spectacular shipwreck of all was that of
he French man-of-war *Magnifique.*

In the year 1782 the great French fleet of Admiral Vau-
aird sailed into Boston Harbor. A Boston pilot, David
Darling, was unfortunate enough to wreck the great *Magnifique,* a man-of-war of 74 guns, on a bar leading from the
West Head of Lovell's Island. Badly damaged, she filled
and sank in deep water, right off the inner shore. Whether
the day was very stormy or the pilot alone was at fault probably will never be known, but David Darling lost his job.

It was a sad day for the new republic when Darling's pilot-
ing carried the vessel to her doom, for America felt obliged

to give France as compensation her own 74-gun ship then nearing completion at Portsmouth, New Hampshire. This man-of-war was launched on November 5, 1782. When John Paul Jones found that he was not to command the new battleship, he resigned from the service, and America was deprived of the services of the man who was perhaps her greatest naval hero. Thus we have the apparent carelessness of a young Boston pilot contributing to the final chapter in the career of a great commander. David Darling, the unfortunate pilot, obtained a position as sexton of the Old North Church in Boston, succeeding Robert Newman. Nathaniel Shurtleff tells us that the children of the North End plagued the poor man by writing in chalk on the door of the church:

> *"Don't you run this ship ashore*
> *As you did the seventy-four."*

David Darling was buried in the Copp's Hill cemetery on September 10, 1820, and the skeleton of the *Magnifique* buried under tons of sand by the storms, tides and currents of the harbor, was quite forgotten by the average Bostonian.

James Lloyd Homer was sailing up the Narrows a quarter of a century later, and as he looked over at Lovell's Island an old man stepped up to him and mentioned the story of the *Magnifique*. The elderly gentleman told Homer he remembered well the day the *Magnifique* went down and he pointed out the exact spot of the wreck. The currents of the Narrows had created a bar over the hulk in the sixty-three years which had passed since the man-of-war went down. Possibly Homer's mention of the incident caused a fresh flock of treasure seekers to look for the gold which was lost with the ship.

Attempts had already been made around 1840 to recover the treasure from the *Magnifique,* but they had failed. Again in July, 1859, excavations were made, but all that the searchers could find were some beautiful pieces of wood from the hull of the ship. During 1868 and 1869 more timbers were uncovered, but since nothing of intrinsic value was found, it was decided to abandon further search. When Shurtleff visited the island, he found that the spot where the *Magnifique* had gone down was not covered by water even at high tide, showing how the contour of Lovell's Island had changed since the 1782 wreck.

Continuing with the story of the *Magnifique,* we move to the twentieth century. On a cool spring morning in 1920, Lighthouse Keeper Charles H. Jennings was industriously digging in the garden near his house on the island when suddenly his spade struck an object that resembled a coin. Jennings stooped over and picked it up. He continued his excavations until he had unearthed many of the round, flat disks. Taking them into his house, he scrubbed and dug the deposit away from one of the objects, and there was revealed a gold coin, worth by its size and weight about $29. After rubbing and scraping, the other coins also proved to be valuable silver and gold pieces of long ago.

Jennings, however, was about to leave the island on his annual vacation, and when the assistant arrived at the light-house station, Jennings told him the interesting news. He noticed that the assistant seemed quite attentive to his account of how he had found the gold and silver, but Jennings promptly forgot all about the incident as he boarded the afternoon boat for the mainland.

When Jennings returned from his vacation the assistant left the island as soon as possible with all his baggage. Walking up to his house, Jennings went around to the spot where he had dug up the coins, and there was a deep, yawning hole. A few months later the assistant retired from the Lighthouse Service and lived in comfort for the rest of his life. The reader may draw his own conclusions.

Just what significance should we attach to the accurate statements made by the Lady in the Purple Cloak? How could she possibly have known of the various treasures about the discovery of which she was so certain? Was it merely a lucky guess, combined with coincidence? We shall never know.

CHAPTER 10

The Chimney's Secret

AN ORGAN, a dream, a spinster, and a chimney. This is a peculiar tale, which begins in a South Shore town in the year 1789. Its principal character is Stuart Alton.

At the age of twenty-one young Stuart was taken into a substantial banking business which his father had founded, and for the next few years he prospered along with the rise of the town itself. Stuart married a local girl, and the couple had three children.

By 1807 Stuart had become interested in playing the harpsichord. During the following year, however, he journeyed to the nearby city, where he discovered a beautiful organ prominently displayed in a music store. This organ, built by the firm of Astor and Broadwood, had been constructed

151

by George Astor himself, the brother of John Jacob Astor, and became a favorite of almost everyone who played it.*

Stuart Alton not only fell in love with the organ, but he desired it for his own. He was only a fair player, of course, but his interest in the organ made him anxious to improve his musical ability, and he began visiting the nearby city and studying the organ with one of the leading players of the day.

Finally, in 1810, his teacher told him that he had improved sufficiently to allow him to go ahead and purchase an organ, and Alton was a happy man when he found that an Astor and Broadwood organ was still on sale in the music store. Three weeks later his instrument arrived at his home, and night after night he would play the songs and hymns of the period. Once a month regularly he went to the city to take a music lesson, until finally his teacher declared that he could do little more for him, for he had become an accomplished musician.

The War of 1812 came, however, and with it a family tragedy. Stuart's wife, returning by sea to town after visiting her son aboard the Frigate *Constitution,* was lost with all others aboard a small coastal packet. The shock was too great for Stuart. He closed the organ and decided never to play it again. To take his mind from his grief and as a rest for his upset condition, his doctor recommended that Alton take up fishing, and the banker would often row out a mile from shore, when the waves were not too high, and fish for

---

* A duplicate of this organ is now on display in the rooms of the Old State House in Boston.

hours at a time. But one day two British sloops came in from the ocean and captured Stuart. Taken aboard one of the sloops as a prisoner, he was interrogated for over a week, after which he was released near Pemaquid Point, Maine, whence he returned to his home.

The humiliation of his capture, together with the recent loss of his wife, affected Stuart in such a manner that he eventually decided to move away from the sea shore, and settle nearer the center of town. Purchasing an attractive plot of land, he renovated the fine old mansion on it. The house contained a remarkable fireplace into which one could walk almost upright. The left side of it was arranged as an oven. Although he never admitted it, Stuart seriously considered playing the organ again, waiting only for the time and the opportunity to begin once more. And so, across from the fireplace, in order that he might play by the fire-light, he placed his organ.

In the year 1832, when Stuart Alton retired from business, he was considered a fairly wealthy man. On the following November the first he wrote to his children, asking that they humor an old man's wish, and visit him during the coming holiday season.

All three children came, with their own children, and for the next few days the house resounded with gayety and laughter. Then, on the final night of their visit, Stuart had them all sit around the fire. He went over to the organ, and began playing it. Of course, everyone present expressed pleasure that Alton had decided to play again, and the former banker was a happy man when he bade them farewell the next morning.

And so it came about that the family visits became annual affairs. As for his organ, he decided that once more he could journey to the city and resume his lessons, for he was forming an unusual plan in his mind. But this time he went to another teacher, a musical expert on composition. Before long Stuart Alton began composing his own pieces. Those who passed his window in the summertime could hear the strains of the unusual organ melodies which he was creating.

In 1851, unfortunately, Stuart suffered a bad fall and was unable to leave the house. Nevertheless, when winter came he sent out his invitations to his family as usual, and everyone came, transforming the house once more by the activity and gayety. Again came the final night of the visit, with all Stuart Alton's descendants gathered in the living room, where the great logs were sparkling and blazing merrily.

Later, as the fire began to die away, old Stuart Alton hobbled across to his beloved organ. All eyes were upon him as he began his first selection. Soon his listeners noticed a strange undertone in the playing which made them uneasy. Then, suddenly, without warning, the organ stopped.

By this time the light from the dying fire barely illuminated the bent form of the aged man, but they could see him faintly as he grasped the organ seat in an attempt to stand erect.

"Children," he began, "I've been practicing in my feeble way on a musical composition which I trust will interest you all. It was written in an attempt to place a special significance on what is to follow. At its conclusion I'm going to reveal something of extreme interest to every one of you and I shall not repeat it. Incidentally, you've probably wondered about why I did certain things in my long life. Well, I think it only fair that you should realize I moved away from the sea because it reminded me of two things. First, my dear wife's death. Second, it was the scene of my great humiliation, and so I moved out of sight of the ocean to try to forget. But I am afraid that I still love the sea, in spite of what I did. Now, I've told you too much already and haven't started my piece. I'll finish my talk when I finish my music."

Already visibly affected by his long speech and his memories, Stuart Alton again sat down at the organ. He began playing. Indeed it was an unusual composition to which the entranced group listened, and as the old man worked his aged fingers up and down the keyboard there seemed to be a hidden message for each of them in his inspired playing.

But at the height of his composition, as he played on with intense concentration, the others noticed that his face began to glow and his breathing became labored. They could see that it was harder and harder for him to continue.

Suddenly, at the very climax of his playing, the old man gave a gasp, grabbed at his chest, and then slumped down between the organ and the seat. His children and grandchildren rushed to help him, and carried him to a sofa. But it was too late, for even as they gathered around him they realized that he had suffered a shock and was dying.

"Come," he muttered feebly, "I *must* finish . . ."

But Stuart Alton was dead!

Three days later his funeral was held in the same living

room, and all who had known him attended. The minister spoke highly of Alton, and mentioned the two episodes in his life which had affected him so deeply. Then the final remains of Stuart Alton were buried in the village cemetery, and his family gathered at the local bank to hear the reading of his will.

Everyone present was surprised and disappointed when he heard the reading of Alton's last testament, for it merely mentioned the house, the organ, and the chimney, and what was to be found therein. There was no mention of any substantial amount of money, except for scarcely more than $1200 at the bank, in an account which had seen heavy withdrawals during the last few years. And the bank's cashier declared that the withdrawals had always been in the form of ten and twenty dollar gold pieces.

Where then, Stuart Alton's heirs asked, could the money have gone? Two inspired members of the family decided to take the organ apart, but they got nothing for their pains except the task of reassembling it again. Then the chimney was discussed. It was supposedly given a careful examination, almost brick by brick, but no hidden vaults or recesses were revealed. Finally the family members swallowed their disappointment and returned to their respective homes.

Several months later business reverses left one of the children temporarily short of money, and he sold his own home and moved into Stuart's spacious residence, where he stayed for the remainder of his life. In turn his son and daughter took over the house when the father died. The son passed away in 1896, leaving the girl, Lucy Alton, alone in the great mansion. She had become a school teacher, and a good one, but her pupils wondered why she lived in the great house all alone, except for two cats.

Strangely enough, Lucy Alton was not in the least lonely, for the woman was fascinated by the ancient mansion. Her father had often told her of the unusual episode of her grandfather's death, and how he had been playing the organ at the time of his passing.

From the time she was a child the organ and the fireplace had always seemed to cast a spell over her, and at an early age she learned to play the instrument. As the years went by she made a study of her grandfather's career, having preserved all his letters and musical compositions which she could find. Eventually she was able to play all his compositions, especially the weird piece with the unusual ending. When Lucy Alton retired from teaching she concentrated on the disappearance of her grandfather's wealth, but could reach no definite conclusion concerning it. None of the letters gave her the slightest clue as to the whereabouts of all those gold pieces which he had taken from the bank.

Lucy Alton was the very last of the Alton line, for the War between the States and the Spanish-American War had wiped out the remaining male members of the family, and by the time of her amazing dream, which I shall speak of below, not a single relative remained alive.

One Sunday evening, as was her custom, she opened the organ. Before her she placed her grandfather's famous composition, which she played slowly and with great feeling.

At the end of the work, she closed the organ, put out her cats, and retired upstairs to bed, but the lingering strains of the music were still uppermost in her mind as she fell asleep.

In her dream, a vision appeared. It was her own grand-father, whom she had never seen, seated at the organ and playing the very piece she had completed a short time before. She felt herself urging him to continue his playing, to finish his composition. And that was just what the vision did. He played his musical effort through to the end, stood up, and walked over to the huge fireplace. Picking up a poker, he entered the fireplace, walking to the left side, where he tapped significantly against the bricks at the back.

Then the dream faded, and Lucy sat upright in bed. Could there possibly be some unusual significance to the dream? She lay back and pulled the covers over her shivering form, but just as she was about to forget the whole episode she heard a sound which made the blood surge violently through her veins.

Downstairs, someone seemed to be actually playing the organ. Terrified, but still filled with a determination to find out if someone was really at the organ, Lucy threw on her wrapper and went to the top of the stairs. But the playing had stopped.

Crawling back into bed, she made a solemn resolve that she would investigate the chimney the very next morning, and fell into a dreamless sleep.

Awakening early, she dressed hurriedly and traveled to the home of the handy man of the neighborhood. After binding him to secrecy, she asked him to accompany her back to the house, and the two went into the chimney.

There Lucy told the handy man, whose name was Jim,

just what her dream was about. Jim smiled tolerantly, thought to himself about the peculiarities of spinsters in general, and agreed to carry out her wish, which was to break through the back wall of the chimney.

But he become interested himself when he noticed something that no one had ever apparently seen before, a certain brick, shoulder high, which appeared to have been reinforced at some time or another, as if for some reason it had been removed and then cemented back into place. For tools he had only several long, thin screw drivers and a hammer, but he had the brick loose in a little more than an hour.

Pulling it out, he examined it carefully. Surely enough, the brick showed evidences of mortar applied at two different periods. Then Jim flashed a light through the hole where the brick had been. There was a small area, less than three inches across, between the row of visible bricks and another row of bricks immediately in back.

Lucy was an excited observer of the removal of the brick and the finding of the space between the two brick walls. But she was not going to get her hopes up too high.

"What can you find in the hole?" she asked Jim.

"It's too small to see anything. Shall I take out some more bricks?"

"Of course, let's settle this once and for all."

By noon only three tiers of bricks had been removed from the chimney wall but they were too excited to stop to eat. At one-thirty in the afternoon Jim had made a hole large enough to reach down as far as a foot above the ground.

"Go ahead, Jim," urged Lucy, "try to find something,

anything. I am getting very nervous in spite of myself." So Jim stood up, rested a moment, and then rolled his sleeve above the elbow. Thrusting his long, bare arm inside the wall, he groped lower and lower. Then there was a faint tinkle as Jim's arm started to withdraw.

"Darn it!" he cried. "I dropped it."

"Dropped what?" shouted Lucy.

"I'm not sure," he admitted, "but it felt like money!"

"For heaven's sake, try it again, Jim, try it again!"

This time Jim decided to pick up just one piece, instead of a handful, and thrust his arm in again. His second try was successful, and the two excited people stared, fascinated, at the twenty dollar gold piece he held up.

"Jim, we've found the treasure!"

"I guess you're right, Miss Lucy, I guess you're right."

At three o'clock that same afternoon two bank representatives were gazing in wonderment at the golden pile of ten and twenty dollar gold pieces which threatened to overflow the living room table where they had been placed. That night the money was counted, put in canvas money bags, and stored in the local bank. Lucy Alton, even after paying Jim $1,000 for his efforts, was $36,600 richer than she had been the day before. And as she was the sole remaining survivor of the Altons, every cent was hers.

It seems that Stuart Alton had used the chimney as a receptacle for ten and twenty dollar gold pieces just as we use razor blade receptacles today. And that was the surprise he had planned for his family on the night of his death. No one had been clever enough to notice the brick which showed evidences of having been removed—no one except handyman Jim.

As for the dream, Lucy claimed that it happened just as she said it did. However, she did offer a reasonable explanation for the organ playing after her first dream. She always felt that she had fallen asleep after sitting up in bed, and had dreamed a second dream in which she heard the playing again. In any case, she was grateful for the second dream, for otherwise, she always contended, she would never have attached any particular significance to the first.

CHAPTER 11

The Sunday-School Pirate Hoard

MOST of us have seen copies of pirate treasure maps, or have heard of other maps not made by pirates intended to lead to hidden gold or silver caches. Unfortunately, for every genuine treasure map there are a thousand made for fun, without any real honest-to-goodness treasure connected with them. Also, for every treasure map which is authentic, and from which a treasure has been located, there are a dozen accurately drawn maps or charts, completed in good faith by sincere, honest men, which have never led to the treasure still awaiting some lucky person.

But the story I have to tell in this chapter concerns that rarest of combinations—a treasure map which led to the finding of a substantial buried treasure.

Captain Bartholomew Roberts was a very remarkable pirate. Born in Wales, he was decidedly unlike the average buccaneer, for he never touched intoxicating liquor, was a strict disciplinarian regarding the other sex, and forbade card playing, dice rolling, or any games of chance aboard his pirate vessel. Regarding religious matters, he did allow his fellow pirates to follow their own inclinations, but insisted that the musicians aboard be allowed their period of rest on the Sabbath. In almost everything except piracy he might have been mistaken for a Sunday-school teacher.

Roberts captured ships and vessels from Newfoundland down to the West Indies, and often sailed along the coast of Maine. On one of his raids he acquired a beautiful, diamond-studded, golden cross, which henceforth he wore suspended from his neck on almost all occasions.

On February 10, 1722, he was cruising off Parrot Island, in the vicinity of Cape Corso, when a British warship, the *Swallow,* appeared in the offing. Commanded by Captain Chaloner Ogle, the men of the *Swallow* were determined to capture and kill this scourge of the sea who had scuttled over 400 vessels in his remarkable career.

But Roberts dressed himself for battle calmly, putting on the most expensive garments in his wardrobe, a suit made of magnificent red damask, and a gala hat with a red peacock feather. Around his neck he placed the costly gold chain which held the great diamond-studded, gold cross.

The battle began, with the British soon obtaining the range of the pirate vessel. Volley after volley scored direct hits on the flagship of Pirate Bartholomew Roberts' fleet, and the cannonading became terrific. Finally a chance shot caught Roberts in the throat, and he fell to the deck, bleeding profusely.

Long ago he had told his men to throw him overboard should he ever receive a serious wound, and in accordance with his announced wishes, they picked him up to carry out their mission. As Roberts was being taken to the rail, Lieutenant Kennedy, his mate, snatched the massive diamond-studded cross from around Roberts' neck, and ran below with it, just as Roberts' body splashed into the sea.

With their leader gone, the pirates shouted across to the British for quarter. They surrendered one by one, all except Lieutenant Kennedy, who asked for a special interview with the British captain. The interview was granted, and Kennedy announced that not only did he have a diamond-studded cross secreted aboard ship, but that he had been present at the burial of several tens of thousands of gold doubloons, and that he was in a position to barter for his life. If satisfactory arrangements could be made, promised Kennedy, he would guide his captors to the treasure.

Lieutenant Kennedy was thrown in jail with the other pirates, but this was just for appearance's sake. Every pirate except Kennedy was brought to trial at Cape Corso Castle, and later hanged.

With Kennedy, however, it was a different story, for once his former mates were out of the way, he was taken from jail and summoned before the authorities, with whom he eventually made a very satisfactory agreement concerning Robert's treasure. The authorities would have eighty-five per cent of the treasure and Kennedy fifteen per cent, but he would be allowed to keep the diamond-studded cross.

The fifteen per cent settlement gave Kennedy more funds than he actually needed, but realizing the vagaries of life, he wisely decided to arrange his wealth so that he would be able to live in America should the British Government object to his return to England. Accordingly, he purchased a small sloop, the *Rover,* loaded aboard his share of the Roberts hoard, and started up the Atlantic Coast.

Arriving in the New England area, he lost no time in sailing to Falmouth, Maine, and eventually to the Kennebec River, where he buried what was approximately forty per cent of his share of the loot. He drew a chart of the area, with directions on a piece of birch bark. Later he killed a calf, preserving the skin in the accepted manner of the day. Finally the skin was properly cured, and suitable for use as vellum. Cutting a portion of the vellum to the desired size, Kennedy made a copy of the birch-bark chart, putting a star to indicate the exact location where he had buried the treasure.

Kennedy then sailed across the ocean, and to his pleasure, was favorably received in England, where he purchased a combination hotel and tavern on Deptford Road, London. This tavern had an especially evil reputation, being patronized by criminals of both sexes. Hiding his vellum chart among other personal effects in his strong box, which he secured under the second-story eaves, Kennedy quickly set out to establish a worse reputation for his tavern than it had even had in the past. Soon he had made it the headquarters for several gangs of pickpockets and highwaymen which he had organized and scarcely a man was safe traveling alone at night.

But one day Kennedy rejected his sweetheart. She returned to the tavern again and again to beg him to change his mind. Finally she realized that it was hopeless, and determined to have revenge. Notifying the authorities of the true state of affairs at the tavern, she was responsible for former pirate Kennedy's being thrust into Marshalsea prison. Then, just to give Kennedy his final push to the gallows, the woman found a mariner who had been robbed at sea by Kennedy when the latter was a pirate. Taking the sailor to Bridewell, where Kennedy had been transferred, she watched with apparent happiness as the sailor positively identified Kennedy as a pirate.

Kennedy, realizing that he was in danger of being hanged, turned King's evidence, and informed on at least eight other pirates to save his own neck. However, as only one of the pirates could be found and he proved that he had been forced into the service of piracy, the forced man was declared pardoned and Kennedy, admittedly "an old and a notorious offender," was condemned and executed as a pirate three weeks later.

One day his henchmen were going over Kennedy's effects in the strong box and came across the folded piece of vellum. One of them claimed it, and it was handed down from generation to generation for a century and a half through this particular fellow's descendants. Finally, around 1878, a descendant more curious than the others who had examined the piece of vellum decided to try to find the treasure which it represented. Sailing for America in the following year, he was forced to work and reestablish his waning fortunes.

He was unable to locate the Kennebec River indicated on the chart, being rather backward in such matters, and spent much time in futile quests in other sections. Time after time his limited funds had to be replenished, and by the year 1880 he was becoming discouraged. He obtained a job in a logging camp and was on the way there when he decided to store his sea chest until his return from the camp.

Thus we find him late one stormy October evening, knocking at the door of the home of Emeline Benner Lewis, in Middlesex, Vermont. Emeline Benner came to the door, and the Englishman asked permission to leave his small sea chest in her attic until his return from the logging camp. After some hesitation, Mrs. Lewis consented, and the trunk was placed in the attic. The years went by, and the Englishman never returned.

Young George Benner often called at his aunt's cottage, and every year he asked her if he could open the chest to find out what was in it. The good woman always refused, claiming that the mariner might still come back. Finally, around the year 1900, she admitted that the sailor was probably dead, and gave George permission to open the trunk.

Besides the usual sailor's trinkets, there were a whale's tooth, an old quadrant, a few shells, a copy of Scott's *The Pirate,* and several letters. One letter, dated at Bristol, England, in 1830, was the only clue to Kennedy's home. The most important find, however, was a piece of folded vellum. George opened it, revealing a map of the Kennebec River in Maine, with a star on a small bay. Underneath the star were these instructions:

STAND ABREST QURTSBOLDER BRING
TOP IN LINE WITH HIL N $\frac{1}{2}$M
IT LISE 12 FATHOM N. E. NEAR
BIG TREES UNDER STONE.

The map, according to George Benner, was about 150 years old. The following fall young Benner and a friend chartered a small motor boat and sailed up to Boothbay, Maine. The day after their arrival they started up the river early in the morning, exploring the bank of the stream hour after hour, until they came to a large quartz boulder which glistened in the sun.

The men ran their boat ashore as near as they could to the boulder and searched the vicinity half a mile to the northward, but they were only able to locate a single tree. By this time the afternoon sun had set, so they decided to return to Boothbay to await the next day.

Leaving Boothbay with the arrival of dawn, they soon found the great rock and again went ashore. When they walked over to the single tall tree, they discovered the remains of another large elm close by and eagerly decided that they might be on the right trail.

By sinking their crowbar into the earth every few feet, the two men located a large, flat stone which was a few inches under the surface, and after straining and tugging, lifted the stone high enough to roll it over. Another smaller stone underneath was more easily removed.

There, exposed to the sunlight which flickered down through the trees, lay a cask, the top stove in, and covered with a fine green mold. Excitedly plunging their hands into the rotting cask, they brought up handfuls of decayed wood and discolored coins which proved to be gold! The keg was entirely filled with coins, except for a roll wrapped in badly-rotted canvas.

There they knelt, with their hands filled with gold, stunned for a moment at their find. With a quick glance around to see if anyone happened to be watching them, the successful treasure hunters threw the treasure coin by coin into the new canvas bags which they had brought along, and after several hours of laborious toil, transported their find down to the shore and aboard their craft.

They were extremely nervous about having such wealth in their possession and agreed that, if the weather held clear, their safest plan would be to stock up with gasoline and provisions and head right out into the open sea, bound for Boston. Thus they would avoid embarrassing questions.

Starting down the coast early the next morning, they reached Portsmouth before nightfall, and the following evening were tied up at Northern Avenue Public Landing. After sleeping on the boat that night, early the next morning they hired a team to transport the gold to a local Boston bank.

Working overtime, experts examined the gold and counted the amazing hoard. Then they unwrapped the rotting canvas roll, and there was revealed a pearl necklace and the diamond-studded cross of Captain Bartholomew Roberts.

The bank finally reported that the sum of $20,000 awaited the two men, an amount which they divided equally. Benner's friend finished college with part of his share, but lost the remainder of his money through stock manipulations. George Frederick Benner for many years was the genial custodian of the Marine Museum of the Old State House, in Boston, where he gave pleasure to thousands of yearly visitors. Now retired, he is still active at the age of ninety-two.

CHAPTER 12

They Found Treasure

MANY persons who fail to discover treasure themselves develop the mistaken opinion that few treasures have ever been found. Exactly the opposite is true. In this chapter I have gathered more than thirty individual stories concerning the search for and finding of buried treasure, stories which by themselves are not sufficiently detailed for separate chapters, but because of their interest and importance, have been included in the book.

Incidentally, many popular misconceptions about treasure trove exist. There are some hard and fast rules regarding treasure in the United States which differ widely from the treasure trove rules of the British Empire. The name treasure trove itself can be applied to any gold or silver in plate, bullion, or coin found concealed *in* the earth—or in a house or other private place—but not lying *on* the earth. If the original owner of the treasure is unknown, title to treasure trove belongs to the finder. The owner of the ground in which the treasure is found has no claim whatsoever to any treasure on the property by virtue of his ownership of the land. If a group of persons find treasure, each person shares equally in the proceeds of the venture, but each is under obligation to keep his share of the treasure for a reasonable length of time against the day when the rightful owner may possibly appear.

An actual example of the working of this American law took place in New Vineyard, Maine, when a man named Leonard Hackett hired three boys to help him clean up his yard after a fire of minor nature had swept part of the estate. The fire had damaged a small building, and the boys were digging out gravel and stones near the building when Hackett noticed one of the boys cleaning around a small can which appeared embedded in the soil.

The boy, Morton by name, dug around the can and lifted it from the ground, whereupon the bottom fell out, sprinkling the ground with silver coins. Two other cans were discovered filled with treasure, and the coins were transferred to a pail, after which they were taken to the Hackett residence for safe keeping. Later, the boys began to wonder if they were not entitled to a share in the money, which totaled in value $1,284.67. When Hackett laughed them away, their parents engaged a lawyer, and the ensuing case was brought to trial in the Franklin County Supreme Judicial Court, in September, 1907. The results of the case surprised almost everyone who attended the session, for it was decreed that as neither Mr. Hackett nor anyone else had the slightest knowledge of how the coins came to be buried, to whom they had belonged or who had buried them, the entire wealth should be equally divided between Hackett and his three helpers. If Hackett had not been with them at the time, the boys could have divided the treasure three ways instead of four.

Another Maine treasure which came to light many years after it was either abandoned or buried was the famous Baron Castine Hoard, one of the coins of which I have at present in my collection.

Baron Castine was a remarkable character who lived on the peninsula which now bears his name from about 1670 until 1701, when he went to France. Castine participated in many engagements against the English on the side of the Indians, and also established an active trading post at his home.

His residence was a weird-looking dwelling, long, low, and irregular, constructed partly of stone and partly of wood. A fort equipped with twelve guns was built around the house, and the entire estate was palisaded.

Gradually Baron Castine became the most important trader in the area, and the Indians brought him beaver skins by the hundreds. At the height of his prosperity his wealth was estimated at 250,000 crowns. In 1701 he left this continent for a visit to France, but died there before he could return.

In 1704 Major Church raided Castine with his British

soldiers. Among those he captured was Castine's daughter, who was attempting to escape through the Narrows of the Bagaduce River with her family. Probably in the short time before her capture she concealed several thousand coins beside a large rock, at a point on the shore of the Narrows some six miles from her home. She was never able to return and claim the coins.

Almost a century and a half later, this famous Castine Hoard was discovered in an unusual way in the town of Penobscot, six miles from Castine's home. In November, 1849, Captain Stephen Grindle and his son Samuel were engaged on their property, hauling wood down the bank of the Bagaduce River to the shore at a place called the Second Narrows, or Johnson's Narrows. Walking along a beaten path through the bushes, Samuel noticed a coin some twenty-five feet above the edge of the water. The money was lying near a large boulder, in one of the furrows made by the timbers which he and his father had just dragged over the soil. Samuel picked up the coin and identified it as a French crown.

Appearing new and bright, the coin was over two hundred years old. The two men fell to work, looking for more money, and found twenty pieces before night caught them. A snowstorm began that same evening and they were forced to wait until spring for further digging. The following April they searched again and found another coin covered with moss on top of the large rock.

Then, a short time later, by the side of this rock, the bulk of the treasure was found. In all there were almost 2,000 coins, money from France, New England, Mexico, Lima,

Bogotá, Potosi, Holland, Portugal, Spain and England. A substantial collection of coins from the Castine hoard is now on exhibition at the Maine Historical Society, in Portland. On a recent trip to Bar Harbor I was able to purchase a single coin from the famous Castine hoard, and have added the beautiful, strangely-shaped piece of eight to my collection.

Late in November, 1901, the British schooner *Union* sailed into Mobile, Alabama, with twenty-two pounds of gold which was estimated to be worth $7,000. Captain Foster told how the gold had been discovered on the sea bottom off Cayman Brac, British West Indies, by a Captain Barton, who was cruising in the vicinity. Barton had launched a small boat and was looking down through the sea with a water glass box, and in only nine feet of water saw something which appeared to be wreckage. Divers who investigated found the gold, consisting of gold watch cases, golden doubloons of the date 1753, and several small bars of gold.

Treasure to the amount of $100,000 was removed from Staten Island Sound in October, 1903, where it had lain in the mud. The treasure had rolled off the decks of a barge some time before, and was located and brought to the surface by divers.

In January, 1913, a laborer named George Hardsook working near Claremont, Oklahoma, uncovered $37,000 in twenty dollar gold pieces there. Later Kit Dalton, a mem-

ber of the Jesse James gang of 1874, admitted that the $37,-
000 was part of a $70,000 holdup when a train was robbed
near Mosscrest, now an abandoned town of the vicinity.
The gold had been buried near a tree, but when the gang
returned the markers were gone and they failed to discover
their gold. Evidently the money lay there undiscovered
for thirty-nine years.

The Maine coast has always been the scene of treasure
hunts, and many of them have been successful. I often fly
down low over Pond Island, at Christmastime, for it was at
Pond Island that the Boston pirate Edward Low is said to
have buried his treasure which he took from the Spanish
galleon *Don Pedro del Montclova*. The treasure consisted
of three kettles of bar silver and a large chest of gold and
jewels.

Captain Low was said to have dropped the treasure into
the pond on Pond Island, Casco Bay, and then to have fled
the vicinity. Later a mutiny ended the career of Low, for
he was set adrift at sea and was seen no more, so he never
came back to Pond Island to recover his loot.

Probably over a hundred expeditions have been sent out
to Pond Island during the last century, and the only person
to profit thereby was the old hermit-king of the island,
John Darling by name. Darling, who lived on dead crabs
and mussels, was the only resident of Pond Island around
the turn of the century. It was said the officials of Harpswell marooned him at Pond Island because he was con-

antly in trouble in town. Out on the island Darling was usually hired to do the digging after the treasure seekers had found the location they felt was the correct one. Darling lived in a tiny shack reinforced with seaweed against the wintry cold, a shack which he had built entirely of driftwood. Usually he would work for fifty cents a day, digging as deep a hole as his customer desired. But as far is known, no one has ever found the Low treasure, although the island is pitted with holes which treasure seekers have dug. Darling died before the year 1928, and his shack was allowed to go to ruin.

Treasure of a strange type was the object of a group of men who landed on Pond Island in 1801. They had been duped by a stranger in Portland, who claimed that he could extract silver from dew. They all went out to Pond Island, but the first attempt failed. Another try was made, with the dew obtained "at the right time of the morning." The mysterious brew was heated, other ingredients were added, and surely enough, when the liquid was cooled, several silver particles were found at the bottom of the container.

The group of men agreed to pay the stranger for the formula then and there, and the stranger vanished with his money. Of course, when the group attempted to produce silver again, they failed miserably, and soon realized that they had been duped by the "Acaraza Man," as he soon came to be called. Evidently the stranger had dropped silver into the brew as he was stirring it.

During the War between the States a pot of gold w
found on Haskell Island, the same place where around 18
a lobster fisherman was said to have been eaten alive
rats who took over the island. The gold, plowed up by
farmer who then owned the island, was declared to
worth $1800. Haskell Island is just off Harpswell Ne
Maine.

At Harpswell Center, Maine, another farmer came acr
gold coins while he was plowing, and found that they we
worth $1100.

There is a small island in the Sassona River, near Ba
Maine, where a hidden treasure of unknown value w
discovered several decades ago. The details of the stor
although known to the older inhabitants as late as 1900, a
believed to have been lost forever.

In the year 1840 John Wilson returned to Bailey's Islar
Maine, with a treasure which he found on a rocky re
which lies between Ram Island and Elm Island. He h;
been walking along the reef when he fell into a hole. I
curiosity aroused, he drew the seaweed from the hole a
found a copper kettle full of gold coins at the bottom of
They were Spanish doubloons, for which he received $1
000 in Boston. Returning to Bailey's Island, John Wils
lived prosperously for the rest of his life, and it wasn't un
his death that the secret of his affluence was revealed fro
papers found in his effects.

Another unusual case of the finding of buried treasure concerns an aged Maine mother. On her death bed she revealed to her son that her late husband had knowledge of a substantial treasure buried on Swan Island, in the Kennebec River, Maine. The boy's father had long known of the existence of the treasure, but because he was either implicated or involved in its burial, or knew something about the man who buried it and realized that it was stolen money, he had always refused to touch the hoard. After the mother's death, the son waited a respectable length of time and then journeyed out to Swan Island, located the treasure without too much difficulty and realized a tidy sum from it. With the money which he recovered he began a fish business, which later grew into a substantial organization.

In the month of September, 1894, a salesman for the Brooklyn department store of Abraham & Straus, J. P. Grady by name, was driving near the Main Street wharf of Greenport, Long Island, when the wheel of his wagon struck something in the road which gave forth a ringing sound. Stopping his team, Grady dismounted at once and discovered a queerly-shaped piece of gold metal, eight inches thick and ten inches wide. The top of the metal bar was actually composed of a mass of melted golden coins, all fused together by intense heat of some sort.

The metal mass was found to be worth about $2500. A possible explanation of how the gold came to be in the road is the fact that during the previous summer dredges had been working on the deepening of the Greenport har-

bor, and material brought up by the dredges had been use
to fill in the road near the wharf. It was there that Grad
found the gold. Years before, it was said, a burning shi
had gone down offshore, and the molten mass of gol
could easily have come from the purser's room aboard th
burned vessel.

On November 24, 1897, Dr. Samuel Caley and Willia
H. Anderson, both of Mount Holly, New Jersey, came in
possession of information which led them to believe th
there was a treasure chest in the Delaware River, a fe
miles from Philadelphia. Dr. Caley had invented a gold d
tector, and was anxious to try it out on substantial treasure
It had already worked on such small objects as gold watch
and ten-dollar gold pieces, and so Caley was ready to ca
italize on his invention. The gold-finding instrument,
small metal affair resembling a hypodermic syringe, w
mounted on slender whalebone handles. When not in us
Dr. Caley always concealed it in a small wooden hood
shield it from inquisitive persons.

A short time after learning about the hoard, the two me
engaged a boat and went out to the location on the Delawa
River where they were told that the treasure chest lay.
seems that in 1866 a copper-bound chest had been brough
to the surface by a dredge belonging to the Tomlinso
fleet. Before workmen could secure the chest, it slid o
into the river, and they were unable to bring it to th
surface again.

During that year of 1866 great numbers of river men trie
to find the chest again; all failed. In 1897 Dr. Caley w

able to locate the chest with his gold detector in a relatively short time. Then he and Anderson hired a diver, who went down to the bottom and discovered the chest, buried three feet deep in mud and slime. The diver explained that there would be considerable work before the chest could be freed and brought to the surface. Dr. Caley and Mr. Anderson returned the following week to find out what progress had been made. Reaching the scene of operation, they found to their amazement and chagrin that both the diver and his equipment had vanished.

Dr. Caley then tried out his gold-detecting instrument, which failed to react over the area, thus proving, according to Dr. Caley, that the gold had been removed. Efforts to locate the diver proved fruitless, and all hopes of finding the treasure were abandoned, for both men believed the diver had stolen their find.

On December 1, 1908, when Alden Barnett was cutting timber in the woods, five miles south of Millville, New Jersey, on the farm of Wilson Banks, Barnett's foot hit a wooden box covered with leaves. Opening it with his axe, he found the box contained a bag of gold and silver coins, with checks on an Albany bank. Barnett turned the box and the papers over to his employer, but rightly claimed that the gold and silver, although found on his employer's land, was the property of whoever found it. The money was believed to be part of the loot stolen several years before by a South Jersey gang, who were unable to discover the place in the forest where they had concealed their ill-gotten wealth.

In May, 1894, laborers excavating ground for the extension of New York's Electrical Exchange Building, at 39 Cedar Street, came across a potful of treasure ten feet below the level of the street. Investigation proved that there was once a famous bathing beach of Revolutionary times at this location. Roman coins, Spanish silver coins, and American dollars were found, but the exact number or value was never revealed.

In August, 1910, sixteen-year-old E. Clifton Witt discovered over $300 worth of golden coins while plowing in a field at Belchertown, Massachusetts. The hoard was believed to be from a box probably placed in the field by an eccentric known as the Hermit of Eastern Belchertown between the years 1840 and 1856, when the property was sold to Elias Chapin, father-in-law of Witt's father.

In the spring of 1897 a quantity of gold and silver coins was discovered on the property of Mrs. Kate Woolsey, of Woolsey Manor, Astoria, Long Island. Mrs. Woolsey had employed laborers to clear a nearby beach for bathing, and under one large boulder a hoard of gold and silver coins was discovered. The date on the oldest coin was 1120, and on the newest, 1561. The collection included an Elizabethan shilling; a half groat of Ethelred, Saxon King of England; a 1547 coin minted during the reign of Albert of Prussia; and a golden coin of Ferdinand and Isabella of Spain.

In or about the year 1905 excavations were being made in the cellar of a Philadelphia business block, when a heavy

oin about the size of a half dollar was uncovered. The
orkman who uncovered it hoped that he might get a can
f beer in exchange for the coin, but the tavern keeper
efused his request. The laborer parted with the coin later
or a small amount. In the course of time the piece of
oney was cleaned and presented to a Philadelphia coin
ealer, who identified it at once as one of the very rare
787 New York Gold Doubloons.

Without hesitation, the coin dealer paid $600 for the
oubloon and it was later resold to a famous collector of
lbany, New York. It is now claimed that the coin is
orth about $7000, for when it was sold with the Stickney
ollection in 1907 it was said to have brought $6200.

On April 18, 1913, a Chicago manufacturer named E. C.
ole deposited in a Chicago safety deposit vault a chunk
f melted gold worth about $800 and weighing two and a
alf pounds. Having found the gold on a tiny coral reef
our miles due south of Miami, Florida, he humorously told
eporters that he had never been interested in buried treas-
re stories before, mentioning the fact that half the popula-
on of the Florida East Coast spent much of their time
igging for doubloons and pieces of eight. "If they put as
uch energy into digging with agricultural results in view,"
e declared, "they would all be rich."

On January 25, 1934, Caretaker Earl Rich of Great
land, Cape Cod, dug up copper and silver coins, two cut-
sses of the buccaneer type, several brass shoebuckles,

bronze spoons, pewter buttons, musket balls and clay pipe
Two of the spoons were dated 1694 and 1703.

A substantial quantity of early American silver dollar
was unearthed by workmen excavating a cellar at the cor
ner of Washington Street and Stockton Street, Dorcheste
Massachusetts, on December 13, 1918.

During the summer of 1914 two large, iron-bound chest
were put aboard the train at Port O'Connor, Texas, by thre
prominent citizens of Austin, Dr. Joseph S. Wooten, J. I
Lightfoot and Dave Harrell. They had been led to th
pirate treasure by Dr. Wooten, who had found a clue in
cave while hunting in the Rio Grande region years befor
Exploring a dark and dismal cavern which opened into a
arroya, he had suddenly come upon a musty piece of parch
ment, upon which was drawn a map of the Gulf Coas
Below was a detailed interpretation of the chart in Frenck
The parchment explained how the treasure of Jean LaFitt
was at a designated spot on the chart, marked with a cros
The document was signed by Joni Benuit, one of LaFitte
lieutenants.

Each summer after his discovery Dr. Wooten spent cor
siderable time tracing down the clues on the chart, fir:
making a careful search of the shore around Rockport an
Corpus Christi, working eastward toward Pass Cavallo an
Espiritu Bay, the latter separating the mainland from Mata
gorda Island. Dr. Wooten then noticed that the contour
of land outlined on the chart appeared to fit exactly th
area around the Island of Matagorda.

For four years, during his vacation time, he searched the island, making his headquarters at Port O'Connor, and taking daily cruises over to Matagorda. After telling the other two men of his secret, he took them with him. The three made a ten-day intensified search at the island, and finally located two heavy chests a short distance from Pass Cavallo. It was a hard task to transport these chests to the launch, but the difficult work was finally completed. Late in the afternoon of the discovery, the Wooten launch arrived at Port O'Connor. The boxes were so heavy that it took the combined efforts of the three men to get them off the launch and into the room where they were to await the morning train. During the night Dr. Wooten stood on guard all night long outside the room, armed with two pistols which hung from his belt and a rifle on his shoulder. Lightfoot and Harrell, also armed to the teeth, patroled all entrances to the building.

When morning came, the treasure was placed aboard the train to Austin and later was delivered to the bank in that city. Harrell returned to the island to look for more treasure, while his two companions stayed with their families in Austin, awaiting the counting of the money, the sum of which was never revealed. Harrell could not find any additional money or chests at Matagorda Island, so he returned to Austin to receive his share of the treasure. Although many have guessed as to the total value of the hoard, it was later claimed by close friends of the three men to have been worth not quite $86,000.

During the fall of the year 1900 a strange band of treasure

seeking fanatics roamed the area around Ashley Junction South Carolina, making the nights hideous with their screams and shrieks. This peculiar group linked religiou activities with their treasure-seeking raids, and called them selves the New Adventists.

Led by Ephriam Grennekar, a former slave, the band always followed the same rules. Grenneker said that the Lord came to him in dreams, showing him where to dig for treasure. The former slave always donned a white gar ment, with a white wig on his head. There was a cross of red on the shroud which he wore, and he carried a staff.

Before the diggers began at the designated place they all remained silent while Grenneker led them in prayer for success. Although the group is not known to have found any gold, they did nearly wreck a train by digging for their treasure on the tracks one night. Several silver pieces of eight were said to have been discovered on one of their strange nocturnal rovings, but of this we cannot be sure

In the month of July, 1903, a group of boys at the Y. M. C. A. camp on Tuxis Island, off Milford, Connecticut, dis covered some treasure, consisting of a number of coins, trinkets, and a gold bracelet. No details were ever made public.

Late in the month of October, 1903, the entire Eastern Shore of Maryland was thrown into a state of intense ex citement by the discovery of gold coins at the Tred Avon River, near Easton. The discovery came about when "Uncle" Solomon Cooby was picking up eels in the sand.

A terrific storm had recently swept the vicinity. Having filled his wheelbarrow, Cooby was about to start home, when his foot struck against what he thought was the root of a fallen cedar tree, but actually was a brass-bound box. The box was in an extremely decayed state, held together only by its brass binding.

When Uncle Solomon tried to lift the box it broke apart, and a golden coin fell to the ground. Taking his coin to the Easton bank, Solomon discovered that it was worth a considerable sum of money. Meanwhile, however, word of the discovery got around and when Uncle Solomon returned to the scene of his find there were more than a score of others digging up the vicinity. Although Uncle Solomon Cooby found no more gold, many others did, and several human skeletons were unearthed as well. The money was said to have been left by the great pirate, Sir Henry Morgan, who was believed to have owned land on the Eastern Shore.

Over forty years ago Mr. E. Gallegos of Las Vegas, New Mexico, discovered a cave in the foothills, six miles from Las Vegas. A plain tablet was set into the wall of the cave, and when Gallegos removed the tablet he found a niche in which there was a stone box. The box contained Latin and Spanish manuscripts of three centuries before, which explained that a party of French and Spanish colonists were attacked by Indians there and all but four of their party were killed.

When one of the four men died the other three buried him nearby and left a quantity of gold and silver in bars and bullion in the same locality. They requested that the finder of the documents should send to the heirs of the colonists half of the treasure.

After the discovery of the document in the cave, Mr. T. B. Catron of Las Vegas offered the finder, E. Gallegos, $1500 for the manuscript. Nothing further of the incident was ever revealed to the general public, although many Las Vegas residents were sure that someone spotted the treasure shortly afterwards.

A strange treasure story concerns a suicide named Harry E. H. Moore, who in 1898 took his own life in a Philadelphia hotel. Moore left a death note to his father, explaining that he had found a treasure and had hidden the fortune again on the beach in Cuba. The exact location was the "second little inlet from the inlet to the Santiago entrance toward the wreck." The treasure was not sought for after Harry Moore's death, and as far as is known, is still where he reburied it.

In December, 1909, Michael Noonan found $300 worth of gold coins while digging at the corner of Depot and Liberty Streets in Pittsfield, Massachusetts. The coins were believed to have been secreted there by Rudolph Schmidt some time before 1904, when he returned to Germany and died there.

On October 10, 1909, gold and silver coins began washing ashore on the beach at Puerto Celestum, Yucatan, as a result of terrific storms of the preceding week. The coins bore dates of the early part of the last century, and were eagerly sought by fishermen of the vicinity. The Yucatanians said that Pirate LaFitte was buried in that country and they believed that he hid the treasure which the recent storms had uncovered there.

On October 25, 1910, John A. Schible of Gill, Massachusetts, found a bag of silver while remodeling a building on the old Howland farm. Although Schible would not reveal the exact amount of the find, it is known that all the coins are of the period before the year 1850.

On January 31, 1913, at Enid, Oklahoma, a mule kicked John Allen in the head, and Allen promptly remembered the spot where he had buried his savings of $6365, which he had secreted during the banking panic of 1907. He never had been able to remember where he had put the money, for he was injured in a railway accident shortly afterwards and his memory failed him. The mule's kick brought it all back, however, and he dug up the money where he had buried it, somewhat mouldy, but still negotiable.

On June 27, 1913, workmen dug up $30,000 in old Spanish coins while excavating at the Guantanamo Bay naval station. There was no scramble for the pieces of eight, as the Cuban law restricts the finder to a relatively small portion of the discovery.

In August, 1913, Charles H. Villar, Pensacola contractor, found a Spanish treasure chest in the shallow waters of

Bayou Chico, Florida. The chest contained Spanish doubloons and silver pieces worth at least $7000, and was believed to have been placed there by pirates of early days.

In June, 1900, seventy-year-old Steven Marsh made plans to leave his home in Fairfield, near Caldwell, New Jersey. Among his possessions was a Bible which had been willed to him by his Aunt Sarah Marsh, who died in 1874, nine years after Steven Marsh returned from the War between the States. Marsh had never opened the Bible, and was debating whether or not he would take it with him when he moved. It was a large volume with a brass clasp. When he opened it for the first time since he had received it and turned the pages, he found that the book was filled with paper currency.

In the pages were shinplasters, paper money of denominations between 10 cents and 50 cents, and bills ranging from one dollar to twenty.

Marsh took the fortune down to the bank, where he was told the total value was $4,867.30. Marsh left Caldwell for Denver, Colorado, on June 11, 1900, his Bible and his newfound wealth with him.

CHAPTER 13

Fisherman Doane's Lucky Night

E ARLY in the last century, pirates were very active off the shores of southern Florida and in the West Indies. Many of them later moved to the United States and established themselves in other fields of endeavor.

Chatham, Massachusetts, exposed to the sea as it is, has numerous sand bars and long stretches of land which make it ideally suited as the burial place of treasure of various sizes and value, and the true story I am about to tell concerns that well-known Cape Cod town.

In the period of which I speak John Eldridge ran a successful tailoring business. He was known to all the residents as an honest and hardworking person. One day a friend,

Arthur Doane, came into the shop and asked Eldridge if he were busy.

"Why, yes," was the answer, "but come in back with me. I'm cutting out a suit." Doane accompanied the tailor to the rear of his establishment, where Eldridge resumed his task of cutting the woolen cloth spread on the large table provided for the purpose.

Arthur Doane seemed particularly attentive as he watched the huge scissors in the capable hands of his friend describing their pattern on the cloth. He seemed strangely restless, too, but Cape Cod fashion, Eldridge didn't query him needlessly, knowing that his friend would come to the point sooner or later. Finally Arthur Doane, who was a fisherman by trade, asked a question.

"Is—is it possible to change foreign coins into—into American money?" faltered Doane in a tense voice.

"Why, yes, there are places in both Boston and Philadelphia, where I go for my cloth," answered the surprised tailor. "Why do you ask?"

"I have a reason," responded the now excited fisherman, who thereupon lapsed into a stony silence.

John Eldridge bided his time, waiting for the thoughts which seemed to have frozen inside Arthur to thaw and break out. Finally Doane seemed to decide his course and reaching into one of his pockets, he brought out a coin About the size of a half dollar, it was made of gold. Holding it carefully between the thumb and forefinger of his right hand, he rapped its edge significantly on the cutting table.

"Can you do anything with this?" Arthur queried. He

was trembling now, the excitement causing small beads of perspiration to come out on his brow. "Can you turn it into American money?"

Laying aside his scissors, Eldridge took the gold piece and examined it carefully. It was a Spanish coin. He turned it over slowly and then handed it back to the fisherman, who now appeared to be sorry that he had revealed his secret.

"Why, yes, I can cash it the next time I go up to Boston or over to Philadelphia," said John slowly. "But where did you get it?"

"Never you mind where I got it. Just tell me if you will change it for me."

John stood motionless for a moment or two, his eyes on his friend. He glanced at the coin again, and then agreed to obtain American money for the Spanish piece, whereupon Arthur pulled five more similar coins from his pocket.

"Get me money for all six coins," he cried, and ran out of the shop in a panic, seemingly afraid to trust himself further.

Perplexed, Eldridge watched his friend out of sight, and after putting away the coins for safekeeping, resumed his work. Some time later in the month he visited a coin dealer in Philadelphia, where he was told that the gold content in the Spanish pieces was very satisfactory and that he would receive approximately $12 a coin.

As soon as he returned to Chatham with the American money, John Eldridge sent word to Arthur Doane to come to the shop. A few hours later, the excited fisherman arrived and heard of his good fortune. Taking his money, after leaving a small amount for Eldridge's expenses, Doane left the tailor shop without revealing in any way how, where, or when he had obtained the gold. A few weeks went by, and Doane again appeared in the shop, this time with six more gold coins.

"What is this all about?" asked John curiously. "How do I know that this money is honestly obtained?"

"Never mind that," returned Arthur. "I have come by it honestly, never you fear. If you will change these six coins when you go up to the city, you won't have to worry. You may trust me in that."

And thus the strange arrangement was made, with John going in to either Boston or Philadelphia every few weeks. The weeks quickly turned into months and the months to years. Eldridge made his usual pilgrimages to the coin dealers of both cities, and the prudent men never suggested that they were curious, although they must have been puzzled about the source of the driblets of six, eight, and ten coins which reached them at regular intervals. Probably between $1200 and $1700 a year was redeemed by the coin dealers in this way over a period of forty-six years, making a total treasure of about $60,000.

Meanwhile, Arthur Doane prospered and married. His only son, born in due time, was unfortunately paralyzed. As the boy grew up he was a common sight in Chatham, manfully pulling his withered left leg after him while making his way along the main street of the town. Neither he nor anyone else knew, however, of his father's good fortune which enabled him to add to his income from the fishing business.

In 1876 Eldridge's young grandson, who still lives at

Chatham, was leaving the tailor shop, when suddenly the boy called, "Here comes Arthur Doane." He darted back into the shop and hid in the rear room. Doane entered the tailor shop, deposited a small pile of coins on the table, and left without a word. The boy came out from his hiding place in time to watch his grandfather place the gold coins in his strong box. His curiosity was naturally great, but as his grandfather refused to divulge any information concerning the gold, it was twenty years before he learned the story.

Four years later Doane became bedridden and sent word to the tailor that he wished to see him. Eldridge hastened to the bedside of the crippled fisherman, who asked everyone else to leave the room. Incidentally, both Doane's wife and son had died the previous year.

"Sit down, John," said the sick man, "for it is a strange story that I am going to tell you."

Eldredge seated himself comfortably in the creaking rocker beside the huge feather bed, and waited for Doane to continue.

"You have waited more than forty-nine years for this story, John, and I know I haven't been very fair in not telling you about it before. But gold does strange things to ordinary people when they find it, and I guess I'm just as ordinary as the rest of them.

"When I told you that afternoon so many years ago that the money was honest money, it was only partly true. I probably had just as much right to it as the men who buried it where I found it. Anyway, it is too late to do anything about it. What I called you over for was to tell you the whole story so that you can get the money for me.

"You may remember that day when I brought the first six coins in to you?" asked Doane. Eldridge nodded, and the bedridden man went on. "Well, at that time I was on a banker, fishing out from Chatham. There was a girl I was going with, and I was especially anxious to spend as much time with her as I could. The captain would let me go up and see her, and then I would have to meet the schooner at the North Chatham beach. One night, I arranged to meet the banker at four o'clock the next morning. I spent the evening with my lady friend, leaving her around midnight, to set out on the lonely trip to the rendezvous on the beach.

"It must have been three o'clock when I was within a mile and a half of the meeting place, that I saw a light in the distance. Naturally I was curious, and walked stealthily over to the location where the light was. I soon heard the sound of voices speaking in hushed tones, and then the rattle of picks and shovels.

"Lying on my stomach and straining to look through the darkness, I could see that there were several ruffians shoveling sand into a partly-filled hole as fast as they could. They seemed to be talking in a foreign language, and only one man appeared to be an American. Greatly excited by this time, I had hopes that they had been burying something of value in the sand. Otherwise why should they choose such a lonely location where no one would bother them, and go there in the middle of the night?"

Arthur Doane went on with his story, pausing now and

then to take teaspoonfuls of cough medicine. He told how the men finished smoothing over the sand and then started away, taking their lantern with them. He remained near the filled-in hole, too interested in what they had buried to leave. Even after four o'clock arrived he decided to forget the fishing boat and let his shipmates sail away to the Banks without him.

Daylight found him huddled behind a low clump of bushes, peering out on the ocean, where two schooners were visible. His own vessel, hull down, was rapidly disappearing, while another schooner, of a type rarely seen in northern waters, was slowly making her way from the vicinity of the beach, evidently with the men who had buried the treasure aboard.

Waiting an hour, to make sure that he was not observed, Doane came out of the thicket and went over to the filled-in pit. He took a nearby plank, and began scooping away the sand. Digging strenuously, he finally struck the hard surface of a box, which proved to be a chest, about three feet long and two feet wide. At his discovery, he jumped down into the hole and started scraping madly with his fingers against the hard edges of the chest. Finding the lock, he seized the plank and forced the catch open.

Doane threw back the cover, and was confronted with rows of bags, which he found contained glittering golden coins. Closing the chest, he covered it over with sand and planned his campaign of action.

"I knew that the safest way was to do everything all alone. So many people have lost out by telling what they thought would remain a secret. Thinking it all over carefully, I worked out what I would do. Three hundred and seventy-five yards away was a great sand dune fairly near the ocean. The crest of the dune was so placed that it was easy to identify. At the base of the sand dune I began to dig. Hour after hour passed. I was so tired that there were times I wanted to quit. Finally, the hole was five feet deep, and I went back and opened up the chest again. Although they were very heavy, I managed to take a bag in each hand and trudge across the sand to the dune, where I piled the bags up at the edge of the hole. Time after time I made the weary journey. It was about noon when the last heavy bag was safe near the dune. The chest itself was my next problem, for I didn't wish to leave a trace if the pirates should come back and dig.

"After considerable tugging and tipping it end over end, I pushed and dragged the great box to my new hiding place. Then I found the hole was just a bit too short, so another fifteen minutes' digging was necessary.

"I was completely done in by this time. Hungry, tired, and ready to quit, I threw myself down on the sand. But in a short while I was thinking of the mass of wealth around me. You can be greatly refreshed by dreams of castles in the air, and I was enjoying quite a few. Half an hour later I was ready for work again.

"The pit was now eight feet deep. I pulled the heavy chest over to the hole and carefully eased it into place. Opening the cover, I propped it up, and in less than an hour I filled the chest with the bulky canvas coin bags, leaving out sixty coins, which I later took home.

"Closing the cover, I secured the latch, and then shoveled

desperately for a long time, filling in the sand over the chest. I was pretty scared about then, for I had noticed two men landing from a dory far down the beach. They paid no attention, however, and probably never saw me at all!

"After smoothing the sand so that no one could tell I had been digging there, I broke my plank into small pieces and scattered it around the sand dunes. Then I collapsed exhausted on the sand and knew no more.

"When I awoke the stars were shining. There was no moon, but I could see fairly well, and by the position of the Dipper, I knew it must be about midnight. I felt for the sixty coins and found them intact. Evidently no one had discovered my secret during the long sleep I had enjoyed. Returning to town around two in the morning, I hid the money in my bureau drawer, which I locked.

"You know the rest of the story, how I came to you with the six coins, and how you had them changed into United States money." Doane settled back on his pillow to rest. When he had gained enough strength to raise himself again, he took a string from around his neck. Attached to the string was a key.

"Go over to the bureau and open the top port-side drawer," Arthur directed.

Eldridge unlocked the drawer and pulled it open. There he found eighteen gold coins. "Those are all I have left now," said Arthur. "When you have cashed them, no more are in the house, so you'll have to walk out on the dunes and get some."

Because of the exertion of telling the long story, Doane was quite worn out by that time. John finally had to agree to visit the hoard within a few days to pacify his sick friend. Arthur then relaxed into a peaceful sleep, and Eldridge left shortly afterwards.

The following Sunday Eldridge made the long journey out to the beach, where he soon located the dune, which he identified correctly. He began to dig. He was successful the first time, for within an hour he struck the top of the chest. Opening the cover, he saw that there were seven bags of the golden coins. After removing one of them, he closed the chest and covered over the hole. Then he started for home.

Entering his residence, he poured the golden hoard out on top of his dining room table and counted the money, placing the treasure in two bags when he had finished. The next day he left for Philadelphia, where he exchanged the Spanish coins for $4,300, and on his return deposited the money in a local bank.

After a few weeks he again visited Arthur Doane and informed him of what had happened. Arthur was strangely upset.

"It may seem queer to you," said Doane, "but I don't think that we are going to have any further luck in the matter. You shouldn't have taken the whole bag at one time. It was greedy!"

Eldridge tried to calm the old man's fears, but it was no use. Doane became restless and disturbed. A few days later he grew worse and passed away, the last of his family.

The next month Eldridge planned to make another visit to the treasure chest and remove the remainder of the fortune, but on the very day before he had planned the trip, a terrific storm blew in from the northeast, causing great havoc up and down the shore. The sandbank near the old site of Chatham Light washed away, and many people walking along under the bank found silver coins there.

The discovery of silver coins near Chatham Light made Eldridge wonder if the treasure chest, which then still contained about $25,000 in gold, was safe from the ravages of the sea. Hurrying out to the sand dunes, he saw with a sinking heart that the entire beach had washed away in the storm. Nothing remained of the sand dune at all! Evidently the chest, which was too heavy to wash away, had been pulled down deep in the sand.

Again and again Eldridge visited the scene, and dug in many places, hoping that by chance he would uncover the chest. But he never did, nor did others to whom he later told the story discover a single coin! As far as is known, the chest is still out there, awaiting some lucky adventurer.

Thus the story of a successful treasure hunt at Cape Cod may inspire some reader in the future to try to locate the missing chest, which probably still contains enough golden coins to permit the finder to enjoy moderate prosperity for his efforts.

It is probable that the chest will never be uncovered. Perhaps it will join the much richer cache of pirate gold located a few miles to the northward at the scene of the wreck of the pirate ship *Whidah*. The spirits of the notorious Bellamy, the infamous Blackbeard, and the despicable Low must indeed be uneasy wherever they are at the knowledge of such great sums of pirate gold lying hidden and unknown on the silvery beaches of this mighty Atlantic seaboard.

CHAPTER 14

Beneath the Sea

THERE are hundreds of sunken ships up and down the Atlantic which conceal substantial treasures buried with them at the bottom of the sea, but of the hundreds only a few are known and of those few less than a handful have been visited by divers and treasure seekers. Without question, over three hundred million dollars in gold and silver has been lost off the North American shores, while the location of at least ten million dollars of this amount is known.

There are numerous lost ships along the coast which have been the object of discussion or search down through the years. Excluding the pirate ship *Whidah,* which has already been considered, there are five vessels which hold enough treasure aboard to make them worthwhile objects of underwater research. They are *Le Chameau,* "The Hessian Gold Ship," the *Hussar,* the *De Braak,* and the *Santa Margarita.*

In order to visit the scene where the French ship *Le Chameau* was wrecked we travel to Cape Breton Island, Nova Scotia. There on the rocky shore, slightly to the north of the ruined fortification of Louisburg, is Chameau Rock, where the ill-fated vessel smashed to pieces.

A terrible northeast gale began in August, 1725, reaching such dreadful intensity that on the night of the 25th all the inhabitants along the Cape Breton coast fled inland to escape the direct fury of the blast. At ten o'clock the next morning, when they dared to return to their homes, they found the shores littered with wreckage and debris, the result of a dreadful sea disaster.

Several fragments identified the ship as *Le Chameau,* a famous French vessel of the period. Soon scores of people reached the scene of the disaster, among them all the important officials who could be notified, for aboard the *Chameau* were many outstanding French personalities.

Evidently the wreck had occurred in the middle of the night, and without warning, for most of the bodies which washed ashore were garbed in night clothes. Not a soul escaped alive. Among the 310 who lost their lives were Monsieur de Chazel, the new Intendant of Canada, Governor de Louvigny of Trois Rivières, and the son of the former Montreal Governor, de Ramesay.

Monsieur DeMezy, Commissaire Ordonnateur at Louisburg, declared that the gale had been the worst in the thirty-five years he had been on or near the sea. In the language of the day, the storm was so violent and intense that "not even a pig came ashore alive." All along the coast from Grand Lorambec to Baleine the headlands and beaches were strewn with wreckage. In its midst Monsieur DeMezy found a beautiful figurehead which he easily recognized as coming from *Le Chameau.*

During my visit to the scene over two centuries later, I went down on the ledges opposite Chameau Rock and speculated as to the difficulty of removing the treasure which sank with the ship. I was not fooled by the wild rumors which stated that from two to five million dollars went down with *Le Chameau,* for I had learned the real amount which *Le Chameau* carried when she broke up in the storm—coins valued at 289,696 livres, or from $55,000 to $135,000, depending on the particular years of coinage, as they varied in worth from about nineteen cents all the way to fifty cents.

Many divers have spent countless weary, dangerous hours, working on the bottom of the sea near the wreck of *Le Chameau.* The most active expedition was operating there in the summer of 1927, a few months after word had been received that a treasure chest containing the money from the *Chameau* had been brought to the surface in the flukes of an anchor by a fisherman, but became disengaged and sank to the bottom again. Try as they would, the divers never found the chest.

The ship which is best known to me is a craft believed to be of the Revolutionary War period, now down in the sands off Cape Cod, near Chatham, Massachusetts. "Good Walter" Eldridge, the man who built himself a house from the wreckage of seventeen ships and has lived on Chatham Beach more than eighty years, was the one who first told me the story.

He has told me many, many times that he lives within sight of a fabulous sum of money, $7,000,000 in gold, which was aboard the wreck when she sailed away from England some time during the Revolutionary War. He never revealed the name of the vessel, but told me confidentially that he had investigated at Washington, D.C., and the figures which he received indicated all that needed to be known about the treasure vessel. In other words, Good Walter is sure that a British pay ship was wrecked just off Monomoy Beach some time before the end of the Revolution, with the loss of all hands.

Should you ever have the privilege of visiting Good Walter he will tell you many stories of shipwrecks and the sea, and perhaps will explain why he is called "Good Walter."

One day, just to be sure that I would obtain the information correctly, I visited Good Walter down on the Chatham Beach and interviewed him by means of a tape recorder. The following interview was obtained in that manner, in August, 1950:

Question: What do you think about the *Whidah,* Walter? Will they ever find the bulk of her treasure?

Answer: Well, I don't know. The *Whidah* came in quite a little above Chatham, you know, off Wellfleet, and we never bothered much with it up there, but Benny Pierce found fourteen wrecks out there on the bottom when he was anchor dragging with Captain Daniel Webster Nickerson back around 1879.

Q. What about the chest they got out of your ship, or the one on the bottom out there that you call your ship?

A. Why, I don't remember.

Q. The story is that they were out anchor dragging, or dragging the bottom for anchors lost in storms and the like, when they came across a heavy chest.

A. Oh, you mean years ago. Why, yes, Benny Pierce, who went out with Captain Nickerson around 1879, he told me the whole story himself before he died. I thought you meant did they find a chest recently.

Q. What was the chest like?

A. Well, it weighed all of nine hundred pounds, and was copper or brass. You know, they weren't out for gold; they were out for anchors. They got out there over this heavy anchor, hoisted it up, and found instead that it was a heavy cannon. Then they found another cannon, and brought the two of them up to the old wharf. You could run a jackknife up to the hilt in the cannon, they'd been under the water so long. A lawyer named Smith bought them some years ago and put them up in his yard.

Q. Wasn't it Lawyer James Stuart Smith, who lives up in North Chatham?

A. Yes, I guess it was. Well, they went back to the wreck and put the grapple down again and it caught onto something very heavy again. This time it took all the men to get it up, but near the top, just as it was getting in sight, it tore out and sank again. They could all see the chest, about two or three feet in size, and it was so heavy they knew there was gold or silver inside. Well, they'd never thought of finding gold, so they went to Boston, got a diver and he went down, but there'd been a storm, and the diver never found it, for the sand in the storm had undermined the area all around the wreck.

Q. Then there's still a nine-hundred-pound chest out there?

A. Yes, nine- or ten-hundred-pound, awful heavy, for it took all those men to hoist it up, and it's full of gold or silver, Spanish or English money, and it's right beside the ship there. You know, I communicated with Washington, and they reported that the English sent over $7,000,000 in gold for the Hessians, and the ship was lost right off here, with all on board, a hundred men. There's also another ship sunk close by, and I think that's the one with the chest, while the other has the $7,000,000. A thousand pounds in gold would be worth something, wouldn't it?

Q. Yes, it'd be all I'd ever want.

A. Don't forget the other ship outside of her. You know Sam Hardy, son of Captain Josiah Hardy, told me about that other vessel. He said it was a merchantman. I've seen both ships, for the one outside has all the ribs sticking up from the bottom.

Q. How long since you've seen either ship?

A. Well, I don't know, it's been quite a number of years, probably at least seven. Ain't it funny? You know there's a bar inside of her and outside, same as it used to be. I went out there about a month ago and put my anchor down, hauled it and found it was kelp and all that black stuff, sediment, so I didn't go any further.

Q. You went out there with diver Prescott Brown, didn't you?

A. I don't think so.

Q. He was the tall diver. You must remember him.

A. Oh yes, Brown, but we didn't find anything. I told him I'd let him know when the ship came up again. Say, it's a nice day to go out there now. I wish I didn't have all these boats out, I'd go with you right now. That's the way it was yesterday when the men you sent down saw me.

Q. You mean the men with the diving equipment and metal detectors? Yes, they called me up, asking for help, and I sent them to you.

A. Well, they came yesterday. It was a nice day to go. I ain't been myself, though. Yesterday we hollered at them as they went out. That man had everything—metal detectors, spyglasses, and diving outfit. We haven't seen him again, but I don't think he got any treasure. Yes, all those fourteen ships are still out there on the bottom and two of them have treasure. But no one ever gets it.

Q. Why don't you go out there more often and try to bring it up?

A. Oh well, I'm getting along, and if I did find it, what would I do with either five or seven million dollars?

We journey down the coast to Hell Gate for the next sunken treasure ship. Many years ago the Dutch named a particularly dangerous passageway between Long Island Sound and the East River *Hellegat,* which, translated, means

Entrance to Hell." To many a worried sea captain it seemed just that, for the shipping losses at Hell Gate through the years run well into the millions. Hell Gate Passage is still dangerous today, but it was much worse during the Revolution. An average of three vessels out of a hundred were victims of its conflicting eddies and tidal currents in those days.

On Wednesday, September 13, 1780, the new British 28-gun frigate *Hussar* anchored in New York Harbor with what would now be approximately four million dollars in gold on board. The *Hussar* was the paymaster ship for the British troops in America. Of course the transportation of such a huge sum was kept secret, and the English denied that a treasure was aboard.

The *Hussar* weighed anchor and sailed for Hell Gate but struck Pot Rock in the passage and began to sink almost immediately. She kept afloat until reaching a location off Port Morris, where she went down in sixteen fathoms. It is said that, in an effort to keep her afloat, the frigate was tied by a long hawser to a tree on the shore and that when she went down she pulled the tree out by the roots. The next morning only the topmasts of the proud *Hussar* showed above water.

Salvage work began at once, but little of value was recovered. The *Hussar* was easy to find on the bottom because of the twenty-eight guns which would still identify her today for an ambitious treasure seeker. (It is only fair to issue warning that several expeditions have tried and failed to find the *Hussar's* gold.)

When the War of 1812 came, the British Admiralty office

announced that, contrary to the belief of the Americans there was no treasure aboard the *Hussar* when she sank Whether or not this was merely an attempt to discourage the American salvors is another question. At any rate, they continued to work on the ship. We do know that around 1832 a British group, armed with a diving bell and other equipment, arrived over the scene of the disaster and proceeded to operate, but the tidal currents proved too strong for their efforts. They finally gave up and returned to England.

The next enthusiast for this British treasure was Captain George Thomas, a character who claimed he represented Jehovah. Captain Thomas, a hypocrite and a rascal who had many illegal sidelines—one of which was the handling of contraband snuff. The captain sold stock in the company he organized for salvaging the *Hussar's* treasure and chartered a steamer which he equipped with dredges. Each morning before the work started, Captain Thomas, his white whiskers shining in the sunlight, opened his Bible and read appropriate passages to his group. Then the work for the day began.

Unfortunately, Captain Thomas was soon in trouble with the Government. He had entered into an agreement with the Treasury Department whereby Judge Nelson Cross would become the receiver for the treasure. Judge Cross eventually had the Treasury Department's agreement with Thomas nullified and appeared as the backer of the new company himself, but he failed to find the treasure. Several other groups were later organized for the same purpose but eventually they all withdrew and gave up the salvaging of the *Hussar* as a hopeless task.

In 1937 Simon Lake, the noted submarine inventor, perfected a device which he believed would allow him to obtain millions of dollars from the hull of the *Hussar*. It was a long, enclosed diving staircase in which he was able to walk right down to the bottom of New York Bay. With the use of this staircase Lake's divers explored the entire area without finding a trace of the *Hussar*. After comparing old and new charts of the vicinity, Lake came to the conclusion that the location has been so changed by the advance of New York's shoreline, that it would be impossible to know where the *Hussar* lies today. In spite of this, the fact remains that the treasure has never been found, and so it must be there at the present time.

The next possibility in our list of sunken treasure ships takes us off the coast of Lewes, Delaware, where there are upwards of one hundred wrecks on the sea bottom. One of those vessels, however, contains a sizable amount of treasure, and the treasure has been eagerly sought down through the years.

Without question, she sank beneath the waves on May 23, 1798, but whether she is worth another expedition is doubtful. Up to 1950, fourteen expeditions have tried in vain to bring up the treasure.

When I was in London in 1942, I attempted to find definite evidence that there had been a great treasure aboard the former Dutch vessel when she foundered in 1798. All I could discover, however, was that the vessel had been cap-

tured from the French, who in turn acquired it from Hol
land. Built in the year 1787, the *De Braak* had been capture
by the British in the Firth of Forth, August 20, 1795.

On May 23, 1798, after capturing the Spanish ship *Franc*
Xavier, the *De Braak* sailed into an anchorage at Cap
Henlopen. She was believed to be heavily overloaded wit
gold, silver, and a vast quantity of copper, which was pile
on deck. The sloop sailed into her anchorage under reefe
topsail and mainsail, and a boat stood by to take the captai
and several members of the crew ashore at Lewes.

Suddenly there was a sharp, vigorous gust of wind, an
the *De Braak* heeled over on her beam ends. Seventy ton
of copper slid across the deck, the sloop filled and sank
and thirty-five men drowned. Another fifty-three floate
free from the ship, and were saved. When the sloop settle
in eighty-four feet of water, the survivors clung to the uppe
rigging, which protruded above the surface. Life saver
from Lewes went out to the scene of the disaster, and on
by one the British sailors were rescued and taken ashore
Later that week the body of Captain James Drew, maste
of the sloop *De Braak,* was recovered and brought ashore
He was buried with full honors at the old Lewes Cemetery

Later, when the captain's wife heard of the disaster and
her husband's death, she ordered a suitable gravestone me
morial erected in the cemetery over the last resting place o
her husband. The memorial reads:

HERE REST THE REMAINS OF
CAPTAIN JAMES DREW
WHO COMMANDED HIS BRITANNIC MAJESTY'S SLOOP OF WAR
DE BRAAK

In which he lost his life when she foundered
at the Capes of Delaware
the 10th of June, 1798
He was beloved for his virtues, and admired for his bravery
His affectionate relict has erected this monument to
perpetuate his Memory.

In spite of the statement on the tombstone, which I copied in the year 1949, the actual date of the sinking of the *De Braak* was May 23, 1798. Captain Drew's "relict" was not given the correct date.

A sum variously estimated as between $400,000 and $8,-000,000 is said to have gone down with the sloop *De Braak*, but salvagers have not as yet brought up any treasure. Although several expeditions have operated over the scene of the disaster in modern times, they have encountered so many vessels on the bottom that it has been almost impossible to locate the *De Braak*.

Over a century ago the British frigate *Assistance* conducted operations over the hull, without result. Later the frigate *Resolute* attempted in vain to pull the *De Braak* to the surface. The frigate was attached to a half-submerged hulk to try to tow it into shallow water.

Around the end of the last century, a number of salvage companies tried to locate the *De Braak* and its gold. Knowing that the sloop had been built of teakwood, the salvagers believed that they were on the right track when the divers brought up timbers of that variety. Suction dredges were employed to bring the gold to the surface, but they failed completely.

There are two sea captains of modern times who have

made noteworthy efforts to find the *De Braak* treasure
Captain Jefferson Townsend of Somers Point, New Jersey
located what is believed to be the old salvaging chain used
by the *Assistance* a century before. But he didn't find a
penny in treasure, and he soon exhausted his funds and gave
up the effort.

The other recent treasure seeker, a resident of Bayonne
New Jersey, succeeded several years ago in bringing to the
surface one of the old cannons with teakwood fittings from
the *De Braak*. When I discussed the matter with him in
July, 1949, he expressed the feeling that he was on the verge
of discoveries of a more important nature when the venture
was discontinued.

"Only one other man and I know just where the *De Braak*
lies at the bottom of the sea off Lewes," he told me. "She is
in eighty-five feet of water. Now don't put my name in
your book, for I don't want a lot of amateur treasure seekers
pestering the life out of me. Remember, no names!"

This sea captain told me later that there was a third member
of the group who had known of the *De Braak's* location
but that he was accidentally killed at the scene of the operations.
Just what the circumstances were which led to his
death I did not discover.

Our final visit in this chapter takes us to Florida. Not far
from the warm waters in which thousands of bathers disport
at Palm Beach is one of the most valuable treasure ships of
all times. It is the famous Spanish galleon *Santa Margarita*
which slid over a reef to her doom in the year 1595. Her
cargo consisted of silver bullion, now worth at least $3,000,

ooo. Located in the present century by a diver who was repairing submarine cable, the hull of the *Santa Margarita* was found to be rotted away and heavily encrusted with shells and marine growth. Giant sharks were in the surrounding waters, but the diver persisted until he had assured himself that there was still treasure aboard the *Santa Margarita*.

The diver made cautious check marks on his own private charts of the vicinity. Then he left the location and proceeded to put away all the money he could save for the purpose of forming an expedition of his own. Several years later he returned, found the ship as he had left it on the ocean floor and descended to begin salvage work. Unfortunately, a great storm hit his boat, drowning several of his helpers. He escaped, but all of his savings had been put in the project, and he could recover but little of his expensive equipment. But his most disastrous loss was the chart, showing the location of the *Santa Margarita*. Without it, he was helpless to relocate the treasure ship. He never again found the galleon.

Somewhere almost within sight of Palm Beach the waters still hold a valuable secret. Perhaps one of my readers would like to search for the lost millions from the treasure ship *Santa Margarita*. If he is successful, I'll claim one silver coin as my share.

The missing treasure of the pirate Gasparilla is another mystery which intrigues the imagination. Born in Spain as José Gaspar, Gasparilla stole the King's jewels and fled seaward to avoid capture. By fascinating the crew with his stories of the Spanish Main, he soon won them over to a scheme of piracy, and for the next few years his name terrorized the Florida coast.

He chose an island in Charlotte harbor on which to live and establish his pirate kingdom. Because he built up such a mighty fortune, he was soon known up and down the Atlantic seaboard as Gasparilla, King of the Pirates. His island warehouse was filled to overflowing with jewels, silks, pieces of eight, golden doubloons, bars of gold plate, and silver ingots. He later buried much of this loot in two distant locations, neither of which is known today. One of the treasures is said to have been concealed in a strange underwater cave near Tampa.

As the years went by, Gasparilla concentrated more and more on meeting and conquering beautiful young ladies. When the men he captured refused to join his pirate band, he executed them without mercy. The women he reserved for himself. His enthusiasm for each quickly waned, however, and it is said that every week meant a new conquest. By the year 1800, Gasparilla was at the height of his wealth and fame. He was then forty-four, and his power of persuasion was said to be tremendous.

One day in 1801, Gasparilla met his match in a beautiful Spanish maiden whose initial resistance to his advances he accepted as a natural consequence of her modesty. But as the weeks went by and she still remained cold to his self-admitted charms, he decided to serve her with an ultimatum. She was to accept Gasparilla as her lover or she would never have another. Her answer was given in a cold, unresponsive voice: "In that case, my Captain, I shall choose the latter arrangement." Gasparilla, bristling with indignation, stood up and strode over to her. Still she made not the slightest response. Then, holding her with his left arm, he cocked his pistol. A moment later, the gun exploded at her breast, and she fell to the ground, shot through the heart. Gasparilla had made another conquest.

This self-styled King of the Pirates met his downfall one day when he encountered what he believed to be a British merchantman. The year was 1821, and the buccaneer chieftain was then sixty-five years old. He sailed close to the unknown vessel, which suddenly displayed the Stars and Stripes of an American gunboat. A moment later, a volley of cannonballs hit the pirate ship and practically demolished her.

But Gasparilla was not yet captured. Long ago he had determined that he would not, like Blackbeard, be cut down on his own deck; neither, like the luckless Major Stede Bonnet, would he die by hanging. Gasparilla seized a fragment of chain cable and wrapped it around his body. "Death to the Americanos!" he shouted as he leaped into the ocean. José Gaspar, alias Gasparilla, who had killed more mortals than Blackbeard, never came to the surface. His enormous hoard has never been located.

CHAPTER 15

The Skull's Revelation

SHORTLY after the middle of the last century George Hawley retired from the sea and bought a small house just across the line from Fairfield, Connecticut, on Long Island Sound. He and his wife Mabel were often seen walking along the beach in the vicinity. On many occasions they would reach the shore just across from the terrible Penfield Reef, the shoal which through the years has claimed many staunch vessels, and taken the lives of over a hundred sailors.

George often brought home unusual pieces of driftwood, which he would burn in the evening, and he enjoyed sitting with his wife as they watched the blue, yellow, green, red, and violet colors from the salty bits of flotsam crackling and burning in their huge fireplace.

One day in 1884, while gathering a bulky load of driftwood after a fierce storm had swept the area, George found a black disc on the beach. Slipping it into his pocket, he carried the driftwood home and then went out in the kitchen where his wife Mabel was peeling potatoes for the evening meal.

"Say, Mabel, give me your scrubbing brush. I've got something interesting here I'm going to clean!"

"Don't you take my best brush now, George. Here, use this old one, and don't clean that thing over the floor." Mabel went back to her potatoes, while George busied himself for the next half hour, cleaning and scrubbing the disc. Finally he stopped, and held it up to the light.

"Why look, Mabel, I do have something here after all."

Mabel took the disc from her husband's hands and examined it closely. Indeed, George was right. The disc was in reality a gold coin, and a rather heavy one at that!

Later in the week he was able to go into Fairfield, where he interviewed a coin collector who told him that he had discovered a golden doubloon rare enough to be worth no less than $45, a sum which the collector offered him then and there. But George decided not to sell at that time.

"Wait until I bring you a couple of hundred of those coins, and then I'll do business with you," he told the collector as he left the building.

"I'll be waiting," came the answer.

For the next few weeks George spent much time out on the beach, looking for more golden doubloons, but he didn't find anything. He would return to the house each night, build a roaring blaze in the fireplace, and sit there dreaming of pirate treasure from the Spanish Main.

One night, as he sat there with Mabel before the blazing logs, a thought came to him. He began to remember, vaguely at first, a story which his grandfather had told to him fifty years before, of an incident in his grandfather's life. Around the year 1822 a group of rough-looking sailors, who probably were pirates, had landed on the beach and hiked over to an isolated headland. When news came of their obvious character, all people were warned to stay away from the headland entirely. Finally the buccaneers, or whatever they were, left the vicinity and were seen no more. Later, through devious channels, word drifted back to the people around Fairfield that the men had actually been pirates, and there were some who claimed that they had buried a substantial treasure nearby.

The story excited many of the young bloods of the neighborhood, and soon they were exploring and digging up the beach in many places in the vicinity of the headland. But when the years went by and no treasure was ever found, the incident was eventually dismissed and laughed at by the people in and around that particular section of the Connecticut shore.

As George sat there watching the snapping logs that night, he had possession of a golden doubloon which he himself had found on the beach. He thought, why couldn't this coin have been part of the treasure buried by the pirates?

The next day he went again to Fairfield, where he visited an old map maker's office and obtained several ancient charts. For the following four evenings he studied the charts carefully, trying to ascertain just how much the beach had changed during the years. Then he went out to the headland and started to work systematically, digging and probing here and there. The weeks went by, and still he continued to explore and excavate on the beach. More and more he neglected his chores around home, anxious to rush off every morning to the scene of his unusual operations.

Finally, one afternoon, his wife met him returning from one of his treasure rambles, and she spoke to him bluntly and firmly.

"George, people have seen you from time to time down on the beach, and I'm afraid that they think you've gone crazy. Every once in a while someone sees you a-poking away down on the shore, or clambering around the hills, digging here or there for who knows what. You're up to something. For heaven's sake, what is it?"

"Well, Mabel, if I'm successful, what I'm up to will make you very happy. To tell the truth, I'm looking for some more of those forty-five-dollar doubloons. I have reason to believe that there are hundreds more of them out there, and if I find them, it'll make us rich!"

"Make us rich nothing," answered Mabel. "If you'd only stay home again and get the house back in order, I'd be willing to stay poor. Now, George, I mean it. You've got to take some interest in your home again!"

"I'm not going to do it, Mabel, at least for a while yet. Give me just another week or so, and we'll be rich people. What if the house does run down a little? Why, if I'm lucky, I'll buy you a residence over near Fairfield, and then what'll they think of my poking around down on the beach?"

But, as the saying goes, the best laid plans of mice and men sometimes fail to materialize, as George Hawley was soon to discover. The autumn of 1888 came, and it was not a good one to hike along the sand dunes and beaches of the Connecticut shore. When the cold weather of late November hit the vicinity, he was forced to suspend his operations for the winter.

Then came the mighty November Gale of 1888, a storm which did terrible damage all over New England. Ships sailing from every port went to the bottom with all hands, and the storm wreaked havoc in scores of fishing and boating communities.

After the gale went down, George made a trip to the beach and discovered that the ocean had entirely changed the contours of the shore where he had explored. Utterly discouraged, he returned home that night and confessed to Mabel that all his hopes for finding more gold were gone. Mabel, worried by his complete dejection, realized that she should give him some words of encouragement in spite of her former attitude.

"Never mind, George," she began, "I'll tell you what we'll do. When spring comes and the snows have melted, I'll get my housework done early some day, and we'll go over there together. How would you like that?"

The old man's eyes brightened up almost at once. "Why, Mabel, that would be fine. Would you, really, go with me on that long hike around the shore and dunes?"

"Of course, I will, George. I give you my promise."

The long winter which followed seemed endless, with its many snowstorms and gales. However, March finally gave way to April, and after a few warm spring days George got up his courage and looked hopefully at his wife. She smiled at him with understanding.

"Yes, George, I haven't forgotten my promise, and I'll tell you what we'll do. Next Sunday, after church, we'll pack a lunch, hike over to the beach, and see what we can find."

But the following Sunday brought a chilling wind in the morning, a wind which swirled and blew across the distant beach. While attending church, during the long sermon, they could hear the old New England meeting house tremble as a particularly vigorous gust battered it. The service ended and the couple returned home.

Mabel took off her Sunday bonnet and entered the kitchen. George, restless and uneasy, walked across into the parlor, where the view allowed him a glimpse of the water, turbulent and rough, far in the distance. He returned to the kitchen, where Mabel had taken down from the shelf several jars of jelly. The coffee was on the stove, and near at hand was the old stone jug which was soon to receive it.

"Mabel," began George, "it doesn't look like a good day for it."

There was no answer.

"Mabel, did you hear me?"

"Of course, I heard you, but if you think that you are going to get out of our agreement, you are a mighty mistaken man!"

"Then you'll go, in spite of the storm and wind?"

"Of course, I'll go," Mabel answered, and half an hour

later the pair were starting their long hike down onto the beach. Luck was with them, however. The wind began to diminish almost at once, and the sand was not swirling around with that biting sting which had been in evidence before church, so that they were able to arrive at their destination a little before sunset. Sitting down on a convenient log, they partook of their coffee and sandwiches.

Then George stood up and surveyed the scene.

"It surely has changed on account of that November gale," he began, "and I haven't the slightest idea where to look for the money."

They started hiking over the dunes. "Let's separate a little and see what each of us can find," suggested George. A short time later they were walking slowly along about a hundred feet apart. In the gathering darkness George noticed something of an unusual nature in a peculiar depression in the sand, but it led to nothing, so he was about to leave the scene when without warning, he heard his wife give a dreadful scream. Then there was complete silence.

"Mabel," he called, "what's the matter?" But there was no answer.

George hurried across the dunes to the place where he had last seen his wife, and there she was, lying silently at the edge of a slight depression in the sand. Evidently she had fainted.

Half an hour later he had revived her and they were walking home together in the gathering darkness. She seemed strangely silent, and at first he hesitated to ask her what had happened. But as they approached their house, she spoke.

"George, go in and light the fireplace, and I'll come in and tell you what happened as soon as I fix up a bit. It was a terrible shock."

Twenty minutes later Mabel entered the room and sat by her husband. They both watched the roaring blaze for a moment, and then she began her story.

"You've got to believe what I tell you, George. It will seem too fantastic at first, but remember—you've just got to believe me."

"Of course, I will, Mabel. But please tell me, what did happen?"

"Well, in the first place, you and I were about thirty or forty yards apart, and when I came to a hollow in the sand I decided to explore it. Reaching the bottom of the depression, I saw something white. Well, you know it was getting a little dark by then, so I took a closer look, and George, it was a human skull! It was terrible, with the eye sockets seeming to stare at me, and the grinning teeth! And then, it happened. It was just too much for me." Mabel began to cry, and George comforted her.

"You might as well tell me the whole story," he suggested, as he gathered her closer to him. "What happened then?"

"Well, George, this sounds strange, but the skull began to rock back and forth. First the skull went over on the back of the head, and the teeth would open, and then the skull would come back, and the teeth would close with a clatter. That was bad enough, but what happened afterwards was worse. I thought that I'd die of fright, and just managed a scream for help when the teeth came apart again, and the skull stuck out its tongue at me. You know, George, skulls don't have tongues. It was so awful that I just fainted dead away then and there. Can you blame me, George? That horrible tongue!"

"Of course not, Mabel, but I wonder how it could have happened?"

Later that night, over the supper table, they discussed the strange event, and George decided that, come what may, he would go over to the beach the following morning and find the skull, if skull it was. Actually, he couldn't make up his mind about the entire story, and who could blame him. A skull which stuck out its tongue at his poor wife! Who would believe such a tale?

The following two days were very rainy, and it wasn't until Wednesday that George decided to attempt the long journey. Mabel packed him a lunch and wished him good luck, but there was a certain uneasiness about both of them, for they were bewildered and perplexed at the strange affair out on the dunes.

Reaching the outer beach, George finally arrived at the location near where his wife had fainted. Carefully retracing his own steps, he soon found the little hollow where she said that she had seen the skull.

Why, there did appear to be something white just showing at the bottom of the hollow! George cautiously made his way closer and closer. Suddenly he stopped, for there before him, at the bottom of the depression, was a skull half buried in the sand!

Soon he could see that it was a human skull resting on the back of the head. He recognized the sunken eye sockets, the hollow for the nose, the high cheek bones, the grinning teeth, and the circular hole at the base of the cranium. "Yes," he thought, "there's no mistake about it. Mabel was right."

Perspiring freely by this time, George discovered that he was trembling all over and sat down at the edge of the sandy hollow.

"This is silly," he said aloud. "I've got to quiet down." Ten minutes went by, and George's heartbeat began to resume its usual rate of speed as he grew more at ease. Then he stared across at the skull in a fascinated manner. How could Mabel have thought that the skull moved, and as for the tongue, that also was a complete mystery.

Just as he was about to rise, however, he heard a tiny squeak, and a field mouse darted across the hollow and into the hole at the base of the skull. The skull swung backward a few inches, and the teeth flew open. Evidently the position of the mouse in his nest inside the skull made the skull rock back and forth. A moment later there was another squeak, and the mouse came out between the open teeth just as they snapped together with a click! Then the rodent vanished again inside the skull.

And thus the entire mystery was explained. Mabel, in the fading light, had watched the skull swing back and forth, and she had mistaken the mouse for a tongue.

Excited at his discovery, George walked over toward the skull. There was a quick squeak, and Mr. Field Mouse beat a hasty retreat away from his home, vanishing over the edge of the hollow with a fast scamper.

George reached down and picked up the skull, handling it gingerly as he placed it a few yards away. Then he took a piece of driftwood and began probing around the spot, until he came across the skeletal remains of fingers and then several human ribs. Replacing the skull, he decided to cover the entire skeleton with sand, mark the location well, and return with a spade the following morning.

That night he explained to Mabel all that had occurred, and she was relieved to hear that what she had seen as a tongue was actually a tiny field mouse.

"And you know," went on George that night in front of their fireplace, "I have heard that pirates often bury one of their number over treasure, to guard it after a fashion."

"Why, even I have heard that story," replied Mabel, "but please don't get your hopes up again, George, for you remember how disappointed you have been before."

"I know, Mabel, but I'm still going out there tomorrow and dig."

Early the next day, long before the sun rose, George was up and about the house. Mabel gave him a hearty breakfast and packed a lunch. At seven o'clock he kissed his wife goodbye and started across for the outer beach. Reaching the hollow, he soon found the skull just as he had left it, and with the aid of his spade, he uncovered the entire skeleton by noontime.

Then he stopped work, took his lunch, and went a hundred yards away to eat it. After a brief rest, he was back in the hollow, shoveling the sand from the area where he hoped to find evidences of buried treasure. But darkness caught him with his mission still unfulfilled. He hadn't been able to dig down more than a few feet, for the dry sand slid back in almost as fast as he shoveled it out, and he was forced to dig away the entire hollow to a lowel level before he could penetrate deeper in the area where he had found the skull.

The next day he was again out on the beach fairly early, but his enthusiasm had lessened greatly. In fact, he was definitely discouraged. Falling to work with a will born of desperation, he began digging. By lunch time he had reached approximately three feet below the level where he had dug out the skeleton.

After lunch George began again, slowly, and decided in his mind to stop for good within three hours, come what may. His back hurt him, and his hands were getting blistered. But he jumped down into the pit and soon was busily throwing up the wet, heavier sand as he penetrated deeper and deeper into the hole he had made.

Suddenly his spade struck a hard substance, and his heart began beating rapidly again. A moment later he had revealed the side of what appeared to be a crock or large earthen jar. Scraping away at the object, he finally had it completely uncovered. Yes, it was a large crock, about fourteen inches high and eight inches in diameter, but the top of the crock was sealed over with a cement-like substance which he could not break.

By this time terribly nervous and excited, George made a futile attempt to lift the crock, and found that he couldn't get it out of the pit which he had dug. He could move it a little, but was unable to get enough purchase on it to hoist it a sufficient height so that he could roll it over the edge of the pit.

Should he smash into the crock with his spade? That

seemed to be the only sensible thing to do. First, however, he clambered out of the pit and looked all around for possible signs of human activity. But not a soul appeared to be on the beach except himself. He leaped back down beside the crock, raised his shovel and smashed again and again at the heavy jar.

Finally it began to crack, and soon a section gave way, to reveal scores of coins which slithered over the sand. George was shaking visibly. He reached down and picked up one of the coins. It was an American ten-dollar gold piece of the year 1795!

George sank helplessly into the sand, his mind completely overwhelmed by the tremendous good fortune which had hit him. But what could he do? Already the sun was about to set in the west, he was miles from home, out on the beach, with a vast sum of money within his grasp. Should he bury it and return later with bags and boxes, or should he carry home what he could that night?

He decided to take back as much as he could with him. Removing his shirt and undershirt, he arranged each in the form of a cloth bag. Then he estimated that if he filled his pockets as well, he could put about twenty pounds of coins in his undershirt and twenty-five pounds in his shirt, with another five pounds of coins in his pockets. The plan was much easier to conceive than to carry out, for there were three types of coins, American ten dollar gold pieces, British sovereigns, and Spanish doubloons. He remembered hearing somewhere that American money runs about $320 to the pound, so he counted out twenty pounds of ten dollar gold pieces, which he tied securely in his undershirt. Then he computed roughly the approximate weight of the doubloons and sovereigns for his shirt.

Next, loading his coat pockets with another five pounds of the gold, he covered over what remained of the treasure. By now too tired to care very much, he sanded over the skeleton, hid the spade, and sat down to rest.

He wondered to himself if he could possibly reach his home with fifty pounds of gold. Well, at least it was worth a try. He got up, put on his weighted coat, swung the two impromptu bags over his shoulders, and started slowly for home. But he hadn't figured on the weight of the gold. Before he had gone a quarter of the distance to his house, he had rested time and again, and each stop occurred at increasingly closer intervals. Fortunately, however, the road was completely deserted, and he had seen no one.

At last he realized that he would never reach home at all, unless he devised a new way of carrying the gold. Then the idea came to him of leaving one bag, going a few hundred feet, leaving the other, going back and carrying the first bag a few hundred feet beyond the second. He began his unusual task, and found that by going slowly he could get quite a little rest while walking empty-handed for the bag which was always back down the road. But of course his new method took twice as long as the old, and so it was almost eleven o'clock when he sighted the lights of his home over a mile away.

At that very moment, he saw the beam of a lantern slowly approaching, and became panic-stricken. What if the person approaching should find one of his bags? He stepped off the road with the bag he was then carrying and hid it behind a stone wall. Then he stumbled back to the other bag, which he also secreted nearby.

The lantern came nearer and nearer, and soon passed the place where he was hiding. By the light of the lantern he recognized his own wife!

"Mabel," he called, "I'm over here!"

"George!" came back the answer. "Well, indeed, and that's a fine place to be spending the night. You had me worried to death, here it being almost midnight and you not returning."

"Never mind, Mabel, never mind anything now. We're rich, Mabel, we're rich!"

"George, are you feeling well?" was her answer. "Come out here and let me look at you. I don't know what to make of this. Come out here, George!"

George stepped out from his hiding place, reached in his pocket, pulled out a few gold pieces and handed them to his wife.

"Now, Mabel, do you believe me?" And Mabel, grasping the hard edges of the golden coins, had to admit that George had found treasure at last. It was a strange scene on that lonely road in the middle of the night as the couple embraced each other for sheer joy.

They never knew just how they carried the gold that final three-quarters of a mile, but they reached home safely. Before going to bed they weighed out on the old family scales no less than fifty-three pounds of golden coins, which they estimated must be worth at least $16,000.

Before the week ended George returned to the outer beach once more, removed the remainder of the treasure from the crock, carried it back home, and found he had eighteen additional pounds of gold, or a total of over seventy pounds in all. A month later his bank account showed a net increase of $21,500, and he was able to build the fine new residence of which he and Mabel had dreamed. Also, he could smile at those who had mocked at him for spending so much of his time out on the Connecticut beach.

CHAPTER *16*

Black Walt's Unhappy Romance

THE story of Black Walt of Richmond's Island incorporates all the known history of this strange man's life together with a fact-founded plot which is actually so buried in tradition and antiquity, that at times it approaches pure legend.

Richmond's Island, Maine, is connected by a sandy breakwater to the mainland at Cape Elizabeth. When seen from the air, it resembles a feathered turkey scratching in the dirt. Around 1900 the government reinforced the sandy bar with granite blocks, piled without semblance of order all the distance from the island to the mainland.

Richmond's Island was prominent in the early days of New England colonization. On one of his voyages Champlain visited it and later described how the Indians there welcomed him with joy. Champlain pronounced the ripe grapes on Richmond's Island just as fine as those of his own France. When Drake, the historian, visited there almost three centuries later it was noted instead for its famous cabbages!

Early events at Richmond's Island did much to make the native Indians vindictive and revengeful. George Richmond of Ireland settled there around 1620, but his career was a short one, and the island soon was taken over by a notorious scoundrel known as Walter Bagnall, "a dark-visaged man, of scant principle." Known variously as Great Watt and Black Walt, he soon came to be hated by the Indians, as he showed himself exceedingly ingenious and ruthless in his dealings with them.

Of course, the Indians had been cheated by certain white men ever since the first Europeans landed in America, but Bagnall's conduct was too extreme for even the red man to tolerate long. Whenever he weighed out material in transactions, he would always weigh with a heavy hand pressing on the scales, and whenever there was an important transaction coming along, he would get the natives as drunk as they could possibly stand.

After they were intoxicated Bagnall would barter for their furs, and when they became sober, the Indians would discover how he had cheated them. After several years of this deceitful conduct, Chief Squidrayset of the Cape Elizabeth Indians decided to take terrible revenge on Black Walt Bagnall. One night he ordered the lighting of several signal fires at dusk, and soon the message had gone up and down the entire Cape Elizabeth area that they were to raid Richmond's Island that night.

Walter Bagnall believed that he still could bargain with the chief, regardless of the fact that he knew the Indians were aware of the many times that he had cheated them. But there must have been a slight doubt in his mind, for not only did he take his treasure of gold and silver from his house, but he also removed from his finger a signet ring which his intended bride had given him back in England years before.

The girl, Grace Thompson, had inscribed a beautiful signet ring with the words, *United—Death only Partes,* and Black Walt, in spite of all his other failings, always wore the ring and kept his faith. They had pledged their troth over the ring back in England, and he had waited in vain for the girl to cross the ocean and be at his side.

Walking down over the bank, he reached a point some sixty feet from the northwestern edge of the small cliff at the island, and put his treasure in a jar, after which he buried it.

Two hours later the Indians arrived at the island in their canoes, and Bagnall, together with his servant John, went down to the shore and met them.

"You know why we come," began Sachem Squidrayset.

"No, I'm afraid not," was Bagnall's reply.

"You cheat our people for too many moons," the chief answered, "and for that we kill you now."

"Why, that's ridiculous!" exclaimed the frightened Bagnall. "What good will that do? You'll just be punished for it."

Before he could say anything more, Squidrayset's toma-hawk silenced him forever. Then the Indian made short work of the servant John. The bodies of the two white men were carried up into the trading post which the aveng-ers set afire and totally destroyed. The Indians took what they wished of the trading post goods and left the island.

Meanwhile, back in England, Grace Thompson was pre-paring to sail for America and her beloved one. Finally at sea, she thought of the few weeks which still separated her from Walt. But there arose a great storm, which threw the ship ashore on a lonely part of the coast and the Maid Thompson, as she was called, was further delayed from ar-riving at Richmond's Island. She finally reached Boston.

Then the day came when a trading vessel was sailing down east to visit Richmond's Island, and so Grace Thomp-son gladly went along. When the trading sloop reached the island all aboard were shocked to find the post burned to the ground, and the skeletons of Bagnall and his servant in the ashes of the house. The ring was not on the burned and shriveled fingers of Bagnall. Grace Thompson was heartbroken, but she felt that if she could only find the ring, she would have some keepsake of the man she loved.

They took the remains out and buried them not too far from where Bagnall had hidden his treasure in the earth. In the meanwhile, the Maid Thompson continued to search through the ruins for the ring over which they had sworn eternal faithfulness back in England. She thought of the inscription, *United—Death only Partes*. How false that inscription had proved to be, for Walt had left England forever the very week she had given him the signet ring.

"All my letters will bear the seal of this ring," he had promised, and Bagnall kept his word, until death. But after a few hours searching through the ruins in vain, she abandoned her efforts and returned to Boston with the others.

Richmond's Island and the trading post were soon built up again and flourished under the skilful leadership of John Winter, who had been sent over by Robert Trewlawny, the new owner of the island.

When Grace Thompson heard of the new trading post, she journeyed to the island as soon as she was able, and obtained employment there. Becoming an excellent worker, she was allowed the freedom of the post. The others knew of her unfortunate love affair, and allowed her to explore from time to time in various parts of the island, but she never found that for which she searched, the signet ring, her only connection with Bagnall. Every summer she would take care of the little plot of land where Bagnall had been buried, tending the lilacs she had planted there.

During the time that she was at Richmond's Island, some four years, the island underwent a great transformtion. Sixty men were hired to conduct the fishing in the nearby waters, and building after building, storehouse after storehouse, was erected to shelter the men and their commodities.

Richmond's Island was soon better known than Portland, Maine, is today. Ships, sloops, and other vessels came from up and down the Atlantic to do their trading there.

It was soon claimed that if you couldn't get what you were after at Richmond's Island, then you couldn't get it anywhere. Many of the old inventories are still in existence in the rooms of the Maine Historical Society. They include the listing of a vast amount of materials, such as flour, corn, vinegar, malt, peas, oatmeal, pork, hops, crowbars, nails, spikes, bolts, cannon of all types, clothes of almost any description, and even boats and sails to sell.

Grace Thompson watched all of this transformation, and thought of how her Walt would have enjoyed it. She took to tending the cows, and would drive them across the bar at low water on one tide, bringing them back twelve hours later on the next low water. It was only possible to cross the bar for an hour at very low water, and after that it became covered.

One day in August, 1639, the Maid Thompson started out at sunrise and low tide to get her cows across to the mainland over the bar. Well-supplied with a lunch, she enjoyed the pleasant warmth of the early morning sun as she crossed to the mainland, and soon the milkmaid and her cows were far away along the banks of the Spurwink River. She returned in the late afternoon, but meanwhile the wind had changed, and a bad westerly gale was already sending in waves which were sweeping the bar.

She soon had the cattle starting across for the island, but when she was halfway across a sudden gust lifted her hat from her head and sent it spinning into the water. Unworried, she rushed after it, but still the wind kept it ahead of her. Finally she was up to her waist in the rising sea, and those who were watching from the island became worried and started out to help her.

Soon she was floundering in the ocean over her head, and the hat still eluded her. A small boat was launched and sent out, but when they reached her she had swallowed too much water. Half an hour later they were trying to bring her back to life, but their methods were so primitive that she died without recovering consciousness.

The Reverend Richard Gibson, the Episcopalian clergyman on the island, presided at her funeral, and as her history was well-known, she was buried in the little plot of land she had tended. At last she was with her loved one.

John Winter, writing later of the incident, said in part that she was a very good servant, and would do more than three such maids as his other girl worker, Priscilla. He ended his remarks by saying that "the maid Tomson," as he spelled it, "has had a hard fortune."

The years went by. Just how hard her fortune really was was not revealed for over two centuries, and by that time the lilacs which Grace Thompson had planted had grown into a little grove. The trading post had been taken over by Robert Jordan of Worcester, England, whose descendants are legion. Around the year 1650 the active days of the trading post were almost over.

During King Phillip's War men went ashore at the island to defend it from the Indians, but were unsuccessful, some of them being killed at the time when they attempted to flee aboard their ship.

In 1705 another ship was captured there from the Indians. Five men were killed by the Indians during the fighting.

By 1800 Richmond's Island had faded out of the picture as a trading center, and farmers and fishermen had taken it over. From year to year the usual stories of the treasure which Black Walt had allegedly buried at the island were old along the coast, but no one ever placed too much faith in them until 1855.

On May 11, 1855, Farmer Richard Hanscom and two of his sons were plowing a field on the northwestern side of Richmond's Island. Suddenly his twelve-year-old son Richard gave a yell. "Look, Father, I've found a treasure."

Farmer Hanscom stopped the team and rushed back to the boy, who was examining an old bottle-necked crock which the plow had turned up.

"Oh, that's only an old jar. Throw it over the cliff. We're late, you know."

"But, Father, I'd like to save it. Why can't I?"

"All right, but put it over on the pile of field stones and look at it later. Come on, now, it's late!"

Richard went back to work, but his younger brother, who had seen the discovery, went over to the jar and started shaking out what was inside. Excitedly he screamed, "Look what I have!"

Both the father and older son rushed for the jar again, and surely enough, there was a shower of gold and silver coins from the crock, together with the long-searched-for signet ring of Walter Bagnall.

The treasure was eventually given to the Maine Historical Society, where I examined it recently in the presence of Miss Rowe of the Society. Any of my readers may visit the rooms of the Maine Historical Society in Portland, and see for themselves tangible evidence of a true story of the recovery of buried treasure. Incidentally, the Hanscoms received a suitable reward for their find.

CHAPTER 17

The King of Calf Island

THE account of the King of Calf Island is one of th
most amazing treasure stories it has ever been my fortun
to tell. As this particular chapter has a tale which directl
concerns the writer, everything of interest which could b
found has been included in its pages.

My first knowledge that there ever was a King of Cal
Island came to me from a man whose name was King
Joe King conducted a business on Commercial Wharf, Bos
ton, and I learned about him while I was collecting infor
mation concerning Apple Island, Boston Harbor. I hac
been told that Mr. King lived for several years at Appl
Island, where he often searched for the treasure suppose
to have been buried there a century before.

In 1934 I interviewed him on Commercial Wharf about
the Apple Island treasure, but he never acknowledged having found any money. However, before the interview
ended, he had told me about certain mysterious events
which had taken place in Boston's outer bay, several miles
distant from Apple Island, where he had lived for a few
summers.

Mr. King told me that out on the Brewster Islands a man
known as the King of Calf Island had been said to have
buried something of importance, either in the foundation
of a fisherman's house or in the ruins of another building.
He wasn't sure, but it may have been pirate treasure or a
clue which might lead to treasure of some sort. The story
fascinated me, of course, and I determined to find out more
about it as soon as possible.

The following year I decided to put into book form the
information which I was collecting about all the islands and
lighthouses in Boston Harbor, and during the course of
gathering information and stories about the outer bay I
landed by canoe with Mrs. Snow at Great Brewster Island.
Great Brewster is a high, drumlin-type island, with two
hills and a flat valley between. A government-built sea wall
surrounds a large part of the island.

The higher of the two hills, at the northern end of the
island, is 104 feet high, with steep cliffs on its eastern,
northern, and western sides, but on the south it slopes
gently toward the flat, level area in the middle of the
island. The other hill is relatively smaller, with cliffs on
the southern and eastern sides.

From the southern tip of the island there stretches an

unusual bar which winds in a mighty S-shaped curve fc
almost two miles, ending at a channel called the Narrow
just across from Fort Warren. At the extreme tip of th
bar, which is known as the Brewster Spit, there stood
lighthouse from 1856 until June 7, 1929, when it caugh
fire and burned down. The lighthouse, which was calle
the Narrows Light, was known locally as Bug Light b•
cause of the seven spindly iron legs on which it stood. T(
day the spindly legs remain, but the burned lighthous
which formerly stood atop them was replaced by an aut(
matic beacon, and now no lighthouse keeper lives ther•

At low tide it is possible to walk along Great Brewst(
Spit from Great Brewster to Bug Light and back in plen•
of time to avoid getting your feet wet. Another bar go•
out to Boston Light, half a mile to the southeast of Gre:
Brewster, and a submerged bar, bare only once or twice
year, runs out from the northern tip of Great Brewster ov•
to Middle Brewster Island. Usually at low water it is kne•
to-waist deep. The bar is covered wtih barnacled rocks an
heavy streamers of rockweed and seaweed.

After landing on the beach at Great Brewster, Mrs. Sno
and I pulled the canoe high above the reach of the incomir
tide. Then we hiked up the slope of the larger hill, whe.
in a little cluster of houses we noticed smoke coming fro:
one of the chimneys. It was there that we first met tl
island caretaker, John J. Nuskey. He greeted us cordiall
and soon we had learned his history.

Caretaker Nuskey was then fifty-nine years of age,
lobster fisherman by trade, and received $10 a month fro
the government to watch over the island where he live

Having lost the lower part of his right leg many years before, he was known as "Peg-Leg Nuskey," and walked round the island with the aid of a cane.

Pulling out notebook and pencil, I commenced my questions about the mysterious doings mentioned by Joe King.

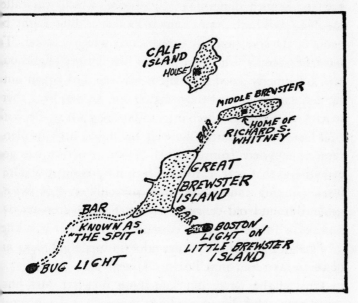

Nuskey fortified himself by taking a sizable chaw of tobacco from his pocket and then was ready for me.

"Mr. Nuskey," I began, "have you ever heard of any unusual or mysterious happenings on this island which might be of interest for the book I'm writing?" John Nuskey thought carefully for almost a full minute, chewing away at the tobacco he had crammed into his square jaws, as if debating how much he should tell us and how much he had better refrain from mentioning. Then we could see hir make up his mind. Spitting out a copious amount of to bacco juice, Nuskey cleared his throat.

"Well, Mr. Snow, it's a sort of yes and no story. I prom ised some years back I wouldn't tell too much of it, but it been so long, and nothing has ever been done, that yo might as well have most of the story now. Back in the se ond year I came here, 1926, there was something unusua Now I've been a fisherman around here all my life almos and got this job in 1925, but I never saw, either before since, a man with steel rods sinking 'em all over the islan wherever he thought there might have been a house.

"This fellow, named Redwell or something like tha came down here from Canada. He had permission an everything, that part was in order, but he spent two whol weeks sinking those long, thin rods down through th ground around old cellar holes and buildings. Before h finished we were all pretty curious about it.

"Finally, I guess his vacation time was up, and he got or of us to take him into Boston. I went up with him, an in the boat he wrote out something which he gave m concerning what he was doing. I have it around som where. The poor fellow had come all the way from Canad for nothing, I guess. Perhaps some day I'll find the pape but I haven't seen it for years."

I questioned him further about the matter, but he wa rather vague about certain points which I brought up, an promised to ask his fishing mate, whose name, for re sons which appear later, I shall refrain from mentionin;

I subsequently found out that the Government had take

ver the island back in 1898, for the Army planned erecting
ortifications there. They had abandoned their plans, and
: wasn't until World War II that the plans were carried
ut.

Meanwhile, as we saw during our visit of 1935, a dozen
r so families had built summer cottages on the island, pay-
ng the Government a nominal fee for this privilege.
mong the families then on the island was that of Mrs.
ertrude Crowley, who lived there with her two children.
Later I learned that Mrs. Crowley's grandfather was
ames Turner, otherwise known as the King of Calf Island,
he man for whom I searched.

For the next few years we made summertime calls in our
anoe at Great Brewster Island, and John Nuskey was al-
vays a pleasant host. We would pull our canoe above the
ide, make a little fire, and enjoy a meal. Usually before
he meal ended Caretaker Nuskey, supporting himself with
is cane, would come limping down the hill. As he hiked
own the beach to greet us, his peg-leg made cup-like de-
ressions in the sand.

There were many things which he pointed out, including
he deep Worthylake well, located halfway up the big hill
nd dug some time before 1695 by the father of the first
eeper of Boston Light. We'd often climb the hill to drink
he water there and as it happened, it was the last place we
ver saw John Nuskey alive.

Then came the month of September, 1940. Labor Day
vas early that year. I was teaching school in Winthrop at
he time, and as my wife and I always tried to plan a long
anoe trip just before the beginning of my educational

duties, on September 5, an hour before sunrise, we were
down on the Winthrop shore with our notebooks, food and
cameras. I carried the canoe to the water's edge, loaded it
and soon we were paddling away for our last day of adventure before the start of school.

Sunrise caught us as we rounded George's Island, and
after visiting several other locations we reached Great
Brewster Spit, at Bug Light. We took a swim and then
paddled along on the northern side of the Spit, finally arriving at a formidable ledge known as the Black Rocks, located close by the Spit. Paddling toward the ledge, we
agreed to get out there and rest our weary limbs, for we
had already covered a considerable distance. I steadied the
canoe while Anna-Myrle stepped out across the bow onto the
barnacle-covered ledge. Then she stood up, her white bathing suit glistening in the morning sun.

Suddenly, without the slightest warning, there was a cry
from the other side of the rocks.

"Say, what are you?" came an astonished voice. "Are
you one of those things called mermaids?" The voice was
that of John Nuskey, who was in his lobster boat, hauling
traps in the deep water on the other side of the ledge. As
he explained later, he had seen Anna-Myrle's head and
shoulders appear above the rocks. Wearing the white bathing suit, she must have presented quite a picture to Nuskey
who up to that moment had seen neither the canoe nor its
occupants, for our approach had been shielded by the Black
Rocks. We hadn't seen Nuskey either, until startled by his
amazed shout when he noticed Anna-Myrle's form as it
appeared to rise out of the sea.

My wife and I returned to the canoe, paddled around the Black Rocks, and brought the canoe up to the lobster boat, holding onto the gunwale with our hands.

"Say," Nuskey began, "it's strange that I should have seen you appear that way just now, for I've been looking out for you for two weeks now. When you get a chance, come over to the island and meet me up by the well. I'll be finished hauling soon now. I've got something to show you." We agreed that after we visited Graves Light and Boston Light we'd return to Great Brewster Island for a rest and some food.

It was shortly after two o'clock that our canoe grounded on the shale at Great Brewster. We had made our circuit of the harbor and were very tired and hungry. I pulled the craft up above the reach of the tide, and Anna-Myrle began preparations for cooking bacon and eggs for our late lunch. But I had been wondering what Nuskey was going to show me, and soon clambered up the bank and reached the well. He was there waiting for me, smiling broadly.

"I've been watching you for the past hour," he admitted. "Boy, you must be tired. You know, I'd never trust myself in one of those things. They look too dangerous, those canoes." We both took a deep drink of water from the Worthylake well, and then he turned to me.

"That gave me quite a start this morning, when your wife appeared that way. It sort of made me wonder whether I shouldn't tell you the whole story. Well, in the first place I found the paper. The man's name wasn't Redwell, as I said, but Tom Redwick, and here it is on the paper."

Nuskey handed me a grimy piece of yellow paper, on which the following statement was written:

> *Write Thomas Redwick, General Delivery Kingston, Ontario, if you find old book on Brewster Island, cover of skin, message inside. In old sail in foundation fisherman home. Good reward I promise.*
>
> *Thomas Redwick*

John Nuskey went on with his explanation. "Of course Redwick was the Canadian stranger, and I found out later that his grandfather was a relative of Captain Turner, the old Bug Light keeper who became King of Calf Island. I found the paper a couple of weeks ago." Nuskey took another deep drink of water, and continued with his story.

"My fishing mate and I always wondered what it could be. We were never going to tell anyone, but we're not getting along too well, lately, for he seems to be getting ugly, dang him. Perhaps you'll be able to figure out something that we couldn't. Go to it."

Excited beyond belief at the actual evidence of a message which told of something buried in the outer harbor, I examined the paper carefully. Then the word Brewster Island caught my eye. There were four Brewster Islands, and why not look on one of the others? Boston Light at Little Brewster would be too small and open to attempt any hiding there, while Outer Brewster was separated by a deep channel from Middle Brewster, connected by bar to Great Brewster. Yes, as I suggested to John Nuskey, it was perhaps likely that Middle Brewster was the island to visit. He seemed to agree with the possibility.

At that moment Anna-Myrle called up that lunch was ready, and so I descended over the bank and reached the fire, where the appetizing aroma of bacon and eggs made me temporarily forget the King of Calf Island and his strange secret.

An hour later my wife and I climbed the bank together. This time I had my camera, and we found Nuskey down by the well again. We talked for perhaps ten minutes, during which period he made the following statement:

"You know, I've been thinking over what you said. I may go over to Middle Brewster and look around myself." Shortly afterwards I asked him to stand down near the well, and took several pictures of him there. Those photographs were the last ever taken of Caretaker Nuskey.

We paddled away from Great Brewster Island twenty minutes later, and waved farewell to John Nuskey. He saluted us in the manner of the sea, doffing his cap and bringing it down slowly in a wide sweep. We never saw him again.

On September 9, 1940, an overturned skiff floated ashore on the jagged rocks of Middle Brewster Island. It belonged to Caretaker Nuskey, but there was no sign of the sixty-four-year-old fisherman, who had then been missing since the afternoon of September 5, four days before. His cane, without which he could not walk, was lying near his house on Great Brewster.

At three o'clock in the afternoon of Monday, September 16, Patrolman James A. Melvin of the Hull Police Department was notified by a resident of the vicinity that there was a body on Nantasket Beach, some three hundred yards north of where the old schooner *Nancy* had come ashore in 1927. Patrolman Melvin went to the scene, where he found the lifeless remains of Peg-Leg Nuskey.

Later, when Mrs. Snow and I read of the strange death of our friend, it gave us a weird sensation, for we realized that we might have been the last ones to see him alive. On October 12 we journeyed to Great Brewster again, and talked with several of the summer residents who were still on the island. I am not even going to suggest that Nuskey's former fishing mate had murdered the island caretaker, but several of the islanders thought of this possibility.

We realized that John Nuskey, had he desired to reach Middle Brewster Island, could not have hiked across because of his peg-leg, but would have rowed over in his skiff. It was entirely possible that he had journeyed across to Middle Brewster that very afternoon of our visit, and there met his death in a manner we shall never know.

I recalled an interview I had conducted some years before on Deer Island, Boston Harbor, with Wesley Pingree. He was formerly keeper of Deer Island Light, and his father was Henry Pingree, erstwhile keeper out at Boston Light. I went through the papers I had saved, and found the record of our conversation which follows:

"If you want a colorful figure for the outer bay, it was Captain Turner, without question. A giant in size, he had a long, flowing beard. He fled down here from the Great Lakes around 1845, and settled on Calf Island. When the Government finished Bug Light in 1856, James Turner was given the position as keeper. He remained there over thirty years, and I think Gershom Freeman, a Civil War veteran, got his job.

"I'll never forget when I first heard about him. I was just a lad at the time, and probably a little fresh. I wanted to hike across the bars from Boston Light down to Bug Light and visit him. Then, when I got there, I stayed too long, and he realized he'd have to row or sail me back home, for the Spit was covered with water.

"He sailed back to Boston Light with me, but before doing so he went over to Fort Warren for the mail. I made such a fuss at his not taking me right back to Boston Light that he decided to teach me a lesson. Just off the Boston Light wharf he reached over, grabbed me by the scruff of the neck, and before I realized what was happening, tossed me into the sea. He knew I could swim, all right, but he never turned around once to see if I got ashore alive! He sailed away to Bug Light, probably rather pleased with himself for teaching me a lesson.

"Father watched me as I crawled up on shore like a wet kitten, and, although he was smiling, he warned me to be careful in the future. He told me that I'd had it coming, probably, but that I should be cautious of what I did in the future in the presence of Captain Turner. He explained that Captain Turner had lost his temper once on the Great Lakes, killing a man with a barrel stave there. Rest assured, I never bothered Turner again. They always said he was a pirate, and had brought treasure with him when he landed in Massachusetts. He came to Chatham first, they say, for he was afraid the Boston police were looking for him. But we really never knew."

Two other clues helped me to build a better picture of the King of Calf Island. Landing at Calf Island one day, I met an old man, Mr. Augustus Reekast, who dated everything from the Chelsea Fire of 1908.

He told me he had something to show me—pictures of the island the way it formerly was—and the next time I met him he gave me a folded magazine story to read about the outer harbor islands, an article which included a picture labelled "The King of Calf Island." I had never expected to see a sketch of Captain Turner, and was tremendously pleased at the picture.

The article itself was written by William H. Rideing, and had been published in *Harper's* for August, 1884. Evidently

THE KING OF CALF ISLAND

Mr. Rideing found Turner just as interesting as I later discovered him to be. I quote from Rideing's comments on the King of Calf Island:

The occupants of the other islands are lobster-men, chief among them being old Turner, who from time immemorial has hauled his pots in the waters surrounding the Brewsters. . . . I do not imagine that old Turner ever smiles; his deep-lined visage is puckered with seriousness, and though he is not talkative, an unexplained pathos speaks out from his eyes, which are screened from the forehead by a bristling pair of brows. He has been so saturated with salt water for nearly fourscore years that he has a half-pickled appearance, and his beard and the curly locks which still flourish, though bleached by age and exposure, are always wet with brine.

The second clue I uncovered at the Hull Town Hall, where an examination of the vital statistics showed me that Captain James John Turner was born February 12, 1803, and died in Hull, March 12, 1888, at the age of eighty-five years and one month. Although the details concerning his father were missing, Turner came from Brighton, England, where his mother's maiden name had been Hannah Cronan. Captain Turner was buried at Mount Auburn Cemetery, in Cambridge, Massachusetts.

I also discovered that either Turner or a friend had cut the date of his birthday on a Calf Island ledge, back in 1851. Later I found out that Turner enjoyed hiking around the outer harbor islands, as he was often seen by the keeper of Boston Light, his huge form moving rapidly along the low-tide gravel bars of the outer bay.

Night after night I worried over the chart, wondering if

Turner could have hiked across to Middle Brewster. Truly, I thought that it was at best an outside chance. On the other hand, the message didn't specify which Brewster Island was meant.

World War II intervened, and I went overseas, returning later as a casualty. After I had reached home again, I was going through my belongings up in the attic one day when I came across the chart over which I had pondered so often.

The war ended and I made up a party and went out to Great Brewster Island with Captain William Van Leer, aboard his vessel the *Charlesbank*. When I suggested a hike across to Middle Brewster, only a few others besides Mrs. Snow decided to make the venture. The group included Dorothy Blanchard, John A. Thornquist, Russell King, Connie Kearney, John Light, and Dorothy Skeels.

It was not an easy day to make our crossing. To begin with, there was neither a new moon tide nor a full moon tide, both of which bring unusually low water. In addition, the waves that day were rather rough. But an hour before low water we started across in pairs to support each other and prevent slipping, and soon were more than halfway across. From then on it was deeper water and we were up to our waists, sliding and scraping along over the barnacle-covered rocks and through the heavy kelp and rockweed. No one who has made that crossing ever forgets it. Time after time the boisterous waves battered us off our feet, and when we arrived at Middle Brewster Island, our ankles and legs were cut and bleeding from scores of encounters with barnacles.

While the others decided to hike around the outer circumference of the island and explore the cliffs and semi-caves there, I climbed the cliffs toward the center of the island, where the Richard S. Whitney property was located. It was my particular objective.

The Whitney's residence proved to be the only building old enough to have been visited over a century before by Captain Turner. When I had called Mrs. Whitney on the phone to get permission for my trip, she had said that the building was purchased from an old fisherman on the island and that her husband had rebuilt the house, modernizing it at the time. Then he had erected a giant flagpole on the ledge above the house. I asked Mrs. Whitney about the cellar, and she said that, although in the middle of the living room there was a trapdoor which led down into the cellar, they had rarely opened it, and not one of the family had ever examined the basement of the building. Of course, there was no known reason for their going down into the cellar.

I went up to the Whitney house and surveyed the ruins. The giant flagpole had fallen across the backwall at the top of the island. I read the inscription on it: ERECTED BY RICHARD S. WHITNEY 1902. Down below it the ruins of the Whitney home stood, the western ell smashed in, every window in the building missing, and the roof stripped of shingles. Indeed, the years had taken their inevitable toll with a vengeance.

Gingerly, I made my way across the kitchen floor to reach the living room, where the three-foot-square trapdoor awaited me. Surrounded by the ruins of what had once been exquisite furniture, the wooden square proved a formidable barrier to my plan of entering the cellar. After fifteen minutes of pounding and prying, however, I forced a corner up, and the rest was easy.

A pit of blackness awaited below, smelling musty and unused. I lowered myself into the pit, and as soon as my eyes were accustomed to the darkness, I began exploring around the area. Then a rat, disturbed from its nest, scampered across my body, and I wasn't too anxious to keep on with my explorations. But after resting a moment to recover my nerve, I continued. It must have been another half hour before I came across what appeared to be a collection of old rags, piled up in a heap in the southeastern corner of the cellar. I kicked at them, and seemed to hit something fairly solid. Could it be another rat? I kicked again, rather cautiously, for in my bathing trunks and sneakers I couldn't offer much opposition to an outraged rodent.

At my second kick the mass went to pieces, leaving a dismembered book, which I gazed at in complete astonishment. My last kick had broken the binding of the volume, separating it into two sections.

What a disappointment! Merely an old book, I thought, discarded years ago by the fisherman, not important enough even to take away with him. But wait, could it possibly be that unknown object for which so many had looked? Could that book contain a secret treasure map or document?

Picking up the two sections of the volume which I had kicked apart, I wrapped the pages in several rags, which actually were crumbling folds of canvas. Climbing up through the trapdoor, I replaced the wooden square in the floor, and made my way down to where the others were waiting. They saw the canvas-wrapped bundle.

"What have you there?" I was asked.

"Oh, just an old book I found in a cellar," was my reply, and no one appeared to show unusual interest. Unfortunately for our plans, I had taken too long down in the cellar, for the tide had gone out and started back in. It was then almost two hours in. We all made our way down over the rocks to the tidal bar, joined hands again for safety, and started back. In several places the tide was neck deep, but I held the canvas-wrapped book high in the air, and when we gained the shallow water at Great Brewster Island the volume was still untouched by the sea.

That night, I carefully examined what I had found in the old cellar. It was a volume seven by nine and a half inches in size, and one and a quarter inches thick. I have it by my side as I write these words.

The outer covering is of skin, said by some to be human. Inside the cardboard-reinforced cover is a statement pasted against the heavy paper. It is signed by one of the consuls on the Island of Malta:

Malta 20 November 1839
I hereby certify that to my personal knowledge this
volume belonged to the library of the Knights of St. John
of Malta of the order of Jerusalem.
Witness my hand on this day and year above written—
Robt Ligetz

On the front flyleaf is written a single word, *Vertiz.*

On the title page of the volume is the following, written in Italian:

L'AMBASCIADORE POLITICO CRISTIAN OPERA DI
CARLO MARIA CARAFA
PRINCIPE DI BVTERA, & C.

Written by hand on the outer skin of the volume, evidently by a scribe in the Malta library, is the following title and numbers:

POLITICO CRISTIANO

~~225~~

352

The volume was printed August 1, 1690, on a private printing press in Mazzarini, Sicily, and is extremely rare, as in the last thirty years only two other copies have been sold in this country. No other known copy at present in North America is as old as mine. Bookworms and rats have eaten into almost half the more than two hundred pages. All through the volume various pages have been corrected by pen.

After examining the volume from cover to cover, I did discover a secret compartment between the recesses of a double page, but there was nothing inside, much to my disappointment.

Later I telephoned Mrs. Whitney and told her about the book, but she said that never had either she or her husband owned such a volume, and by the laws of treasure-trove the book was mine to keep.

I showed the volume to several friends. One of them

who read Italian readily, Robert M. Evans, pronounced the book rather uninteresting, except for those portions especially concerned with procedure in the papal courts.

Later I took the volume to the Rare Book Department of the Boston Public Library, where I showed it to my friend, Miss Harriet Swift. Miss Swift had often helped me in my problems while gathering material for my first book, published in 1935, and I knew that she would be interested in what I had discovered.

Returning a week later, I found that she had identified the book as a rare one, but when I mentioned my hope that there might be a clue toward buried treasure she smiled tolerantly.

However, a few days later my telephone rang. It was Miss Swift, and from her manner she was a little excited. "Come in here just as soon as you can, Mr. Snow, for I've something to show you."

An hour later I was in the Rare Book Department, where Miss Swift greeted me.

"I know that it's foolish to get excited, but I may have something for you," she said as she opened my old book at pages 100 and 101. "Look carefully," she went on, trying to conceal her excitement. I glanced carefully at the open volume, but saw nothing unusual.

"Hold up page 101 so that the light shines through," she suggested. I did so, and except for a few words which had been rewritten, there was nothing to notice. There were about 270 words printed in Italian, but nothing of importance, or so it seemed to me. Concealing my disappointment, for I had come all the way from Winthrop evidently for nothing, I continued to study page 101.

"Well," said Miss Swift, "what can you tell me?"

"Except for a few smudges and a little rewriting of the letters, there's nothing unusual," was my answer.

"Nothing unusual?" Miss Swift smiled. "That page actually contains a crude attempt at a coded message. Study it and you may have your answer as to why the book was hidden. For example, glance at the eleventh line up from the bottom of the page." I did so, and found that the line had been corrected in pen, probably centuries ago. I studied it carefully, trying to read it aloud in my best Italian pronunciation.

"Appostolica. Sceso di poi l'Ambasciadore dal palchetto."

"Never mind what it says," Miss Swift broke in, "for the line itself isn't important. I was first drawn to it by the unusual corrections in ink. You see, *Sceso di poi* was evidently written in as a correction by the printer or proofreader after the volume was finished and bound. That of course is interesting, but not as important as the next word. Look carefully at the next word, *l'Ambasciadore*. Do you see anything unusual about the *o* and the *r?"*

Suddenly I realized what she meant, for over each of the two letters there was a small hole or pin prick in the page itself. Miss Swift had discovered the secret of the book, and there was probably a hidden message pinpricked into the paper of page 101, each tiny hole placed exactly over a certain letter There were about forty-five pin pricks. Whoever had done the work had not been careful, for

baciarà il piede, e la mano, e farà alzato all' am-
plesso di Sua Santità : Poi di nuovo inginocchiatosi
ciporrà brevemente i motivi della sua Ambasciata, e
baciata la lettera regia, vmilmente la presenterà a
N. S., che risponderà con brevità di parole, dopo di
che l'Ambasciadore s'alzerà in piedi, e fatta nuova
genuflessione farà condotto dal Maestro delle ceremonie
al luogo apparecchiato per l'orazione, e nell'andarvi
saluterà chinando il capo dall' vna e l'altra parte li
Cardinali. Giunto al luogo dell'orazione con colui che
dovrà recitarla, farà nuova genuflessione, & in piedi
sempre scoperto aspetterà, che dal segretario di Sua
Santità sia letta la lettera da lui presentata, letta la
quale, l'Ambasciadore, e l'Oratore faranno vn'altra
genuflessione a Sua Santità, e si reciterà l'orazione,
nella quale ogni qual volta occorrerà dire, Sua Santità, Sua Beatitudine, o nominare Sua Santità, & all'
intero periodo dell'vbbidienza dovranno ambi due ge-
nuflettere con rispettoso ossequio. Finita l'orazione,
faranno parimente genuflessione, & alzatisi in piedi
vdirà l'Ambasciadore la risposta dal secretario di Sua
Santità, & il *rogito* dal proccuratore della camera
Appostolica. *Sceso di poi* l'Ambasciadore dal palchetto
dell'orazione tornerà al soglio, e si chiamaranno tra
tanto dal Maestro delle ceremonie li Cardinali nomi-
nati dall'Ambasciadore, tra i quali sogliono sempre
nominarsi il Decano del sagro Collegio, il Cardinal
Nipote del Papa, & il segretario di stato, se sa-
rà Cardinale, nè possono in tanto eccedere il numero
di otto Cardinali. Nell'andare al soglio l'Ambasciadore saluterà li Cardinali, e fatta la genuflessione avan-
ti a'gradini, salirà al piano del medesimo soglio, ba-
cierà solamente il piede, e supplicherà Sua Beatitudine

di

the holes had gone through the back of the paper and through the next page, 103, but as page 101 was the only page where the holes hit exactly over letters, we knew that neither on page 102, 103, or 104 could there be a message.

"Now go home and see what you can discover, young man," Miss Swift suggested.

Gratefully acknowledging my thanks, I returned home and stayed up half the night trying to arrange the pin pricks so that they meant something.

After arranging and rearranging the words which contained pinpricks on them, I worked out a system which eventually allowed me to solve the code.

For the benefit of those who prefer to forego the work of translating essentially what is on page 101, Robert M. Evans translated it and reported as follows:

"Page 101 consists of a series of rather involved directions covering the somewhat stilted protocol to be observed at the Papal Court upon the occasion of an Ambassador to His Holiness presenting his credentials and delivering to his Secretary of State the message entrusted to him by the King who sent him."

Thus I came to feel that there was nothing of importance in the translation of the pages which had the pin pricks, and that any possible solution lay in the arrangement of the pinpricked letters or words. For the purpose of simplification, from the approximately 270 words on page 101 in the Italian volume, I list below only those which were necessary for the eventual solution, the words which were overscored with pin pricks, and I shall use small black dots for identification:

brevemente	Ambasciata	baciata	rispondera
brevita	nuova	ceremonie	apparacchiato
salutera	chinando	occorrera	dovranno
ambi	genuilettre	ossequio	parimente
genuflessione	Santita	l'Ambasciadore	tornera
si	Maestro	ceremonie	Ambasciadore
tra	Nipote	segretario	stato
se	eccedere	numero	andare
genuflessione	del	soglio	

Actually, the secret code was not really a code at all, but merely the simplest form of deception, a form which Edgar Allan Poe or A. Conan Doyle probably would have scorned, but so simple that its simplicity may fool the average reader even now. So in all fairness, I suggest that you do not read ahead for the solution until you have made at least a slight effort to solve the puzzle yourself, for you already are in possession of every clue or help necessary to solve the message.

The solution of the message which led to the finding of the treasure at Cape Cod, follows:

By placing the pinpricked letters of each line side by side we get the following result:

RABR

ETUOMAHT

AHCDN

ALSI

GNORT

SSEER

TTSA

EEUD

SIDLOG

An effort to solve the message by putting down the first letter in each line gets the reader nowhere, so another possibility is to arrange all the characters side by side, as follows:

RABRETUOMAHTAHCDNALSIGNORTSSEERTTSAEEUDSIDLOG

However, the solution still eludes us. Even by alternating the letters, first taking every other letter and every other third letter, we find that the results are neither satisfying nor instructive.

Finally, after many minutes and hours of experimentation, you may try writing the letters backwards, thusly:

GOLDISDUEEASTTREESSTRONGISLANDCHATHAMOUTERBAR

Simplifying the message still further, by introducing the spaces at the proper intervals, you can read:

GOLD IS DUE EAST TREES STRONG ISLAND

CHATHAM OUTER BAR

The next step after finding the directions on page 101 of the Italian book was to act on the information which the message gave. The discovery of the book and its code had been announced in the local papers, and Mrs. Gertrude Crowley of Winthrop, granddaughter of the bearded Captain Turner of Calf Island and Bug Light fame, volunteered the information that her family had always heard Captain Turner had buried not one, but two boxes of treasure, both down on Cape Cod, before he came to Boston Harbor at all.

One day I received a telephone call from Richard Stedman Chaloff, a Boston inventor who was interested in the construction of metal detectors and the like. He asked me if I had ever thought of going after this treasure by metal detector. As I had already sent for one from Palo Alto, California, I told him about it, and when it arrived he tested it in various ways and found it satisfactory, for it reacted to metal from four to five feet down.

"However, Ed," he told me finally, "I can build you a more powerful set, and I shall, some day." I am still awaiting that detector, although Chaloff did experiment with one that gave a reaction to metal six feet underground.

The following week I reached Chatham and went to work, lining up the old trees on Strong Island with the Outer Bar due east, but it was very disappointing. Every fragment of old shipwreck or ship timber in the vicinity had its own metal spikes or strapping of iron, and the chains and metal of various sorts in the vicinity made the hunt harder and harder.

My visits continued day after day, week-end after weekend, but although I found an amazing amount of almost every sort of iron or brass and copper fragments, as yet there was nothing resembling gold.

One night I went to see Good Walter Eldridge, and after that he would row over to visit me from time to time. His eyes would glisten with excitement as he watched me work. He wouldn't offer to help, but would always be encouraging, and when he went away he'd say:

"Well, I've got to go out to *my* treasure ship soon, and see if she's coming out of the sand down there on the bottom." But when Good Walter would return and I'd ask him about it, he'd say, "No, I haven't gone out yet."

October came, and with it the last summer Cape Cod visitors vanished, the people Captain Nickerson calls the "health eaters."

It was a Friday afternoon when the metal detector paid for its cost. I had already hit six "duds" that morning, and after lining up Chatham Light radio mast with a point of land nearby for my bearings, I set out again, slowly and painstakingly walking between the long wooden handles of the detector. My ear-phones on, I watched the M-Scope indicator as the needle rose and fell.

The sun was still hot and strong, and I was just about to stop and take a drink of water when the needle gave a little jump. The hum of the phones increased correspondingly. It didn't seem too important at the time, for on several other occasions the recording had actually been much higher.

I recrossed the area from side to side and the phones hummed encouragingly at each crossing. Finally I had centered the area of activity to a spot a yard in diameter, and it was there that I prepared to dig. Setting down the indicator, I returned to the boat for my spade, and was soon hard at work.

Throwing up spadeful after spadeful of sand, I dug until I was two feet below the surface. The sand kept sliding back in, and so I widened the pit which I was making. Soon my waist was almost even with the top of the pit, but I had found nothing. Whatever metal it was which had caused the M-Scope reaction was still undiscovered.

Resting briefly, I wiped the perspiration from my brow. Eventually I decided that I was ready for another try. But I needed a little reassurance that the metal was still there.

Surely enough, when I tried out the M-Scope, the needle rose higher than ever!

Still, it would do that in any case, if I was getting closer to any objective, be it iron, brass, copper, pieces of eight or doubloons. Finally I was down so far that I knew I'd have to strike something soon, for measuring from the surface I had almost reached the downward limits of the detector's power. Desperately I plunged the spade into the center of the pit, and struck a hard object six inches down. It felt like wood, but it seemed to yield.

I dropped to my knees and scraped feverishly at the sand with my bare hands, until I reached what my spade had encountered,—a piece of rotten wood. Tossing it aside, I came across another and still another fragment of decayed wood. Then there was an entire area spotted with minute, rotted fragments of some type of wooden container.

Grabbing the spade again, I dug in four or five times and then threw the combined mass of sand and rotted wood out of the pit. Holding the spade for another plunge, I pressed it firmly with my left foot, but the spade went down just a few inches, clinking to a stop against a hard, metallic-like object which did not yield to pressure.

Could it be the object for which I searched, or was it merely another spike attached to an ancient, forgotten shipwreck?

There was only one way of finding out, and again I dropped to my knees and began pawing away the sand, digging and scraping until my fingers were almost bleeding. Then my fingernails clawed across the top of a small chest.

At the possibility of actually finding treasure, I fought a losing battle with myself—a vain struggle to keep nerves and blood-pressure at normal level. I was excited and tense, in spite of all my plans to be calm.

Impatiently scattering the broken bits of wood out of the way, my probing fingers were soon surrounding the upper section of the box, which was about eight inches wide and six inches square. Tugging and pulling, I finally released it from the sands which had held it for over a century, and pulled it across my knees. The lid wouldn't open, and so I pried it up with the spade point.

I was not disappointed. There, revealed to my fascinated, unbelieving eyes, was a collection of silver and gold coins, covered with rust, sand, and ancient bits of newspaper. I sank exhausted against the side of the pit.

I had reached my objective! *I had found treasure!*

Two days later, when the excitement had died down a trifle, an appraisal of my collection was attempted. The most costly piece of all, strangely enough, was not a Spanish doubloon nor a Portuguese moidore, but an old silver piece of eight, misshapen and apparently of low value. Robert I. Nesmith, famed collector and writer on Spanish and South American coins, gave me a surprisingly large amount for the piece of eight, which he identified as one of unusual rarity.

In all, the 316 coins which I found in the treasure box were worth almost $1800, not a large sum by today's values, but neither was it a small one. I have retained a number of coins from the collection, together with the Italian volume, which according to several book collectors is almost priceless, being a hand-corrected first edition. I trust that I shall never be forced to part with either the ancient volume or the pirate's treasure coins which I have kept.

Whenever my thoughts go back to the King of Calf Island and his treasure, I still have a strange feeling about the entire affair. There are so many questions which were not answered, chief among them the following:

Why and how did Caretaker Nuskey meet his death?

Why did James Turner hide his rare volume in a Middle Brewster Island cellar?

Where did Turner get the rare volume in the first place?

Why did he bury the treasure so far from his home at Calf Island?

These four questions hold the key to the unsolved part of this strange mystery, but it is my belief that the answers will never be found.